THE
ALBUMEN
&
SALTED PAPER
BOOK

THE
ALBUMEN
&
SALTED PAPER
BOOK

THE HISTORY AND PRACTICE OF
PHOTOGRAPHIC PRINTING
1840 – 1895

James M. Reilly

2ND EDITION

CARY GRAPHIC ARTS PRESS
ROCHESTER, NEW YORK

For Linda, Jennifer and Daniel

RIT Cary Graphic Arts Press
90 Lomb Memorial Drive
Rochester, New York 14623-5604
http://carypress.rit.edu

Book and cover design: Lisa J. Mauro

Printed in the U.S.A.

*The first edition of this book was published in 1980 by
Light Impressions Corporation and is no longer in print.*

ISBN 978-1-933360-78-2 (cloth)

Library of Congress Cataloging-in-Publication Data

Reilly, James M., 1946-
The albumen & salted paper book: the history and practice of
photographic printing 1840/1895 / James M. Reilly. — Second
edition.
     pages cm
Includes bibliographical references and index.
ISBN 978-1-933360-78-2 (cloth) — ISBN 978-1-933360-79-9 (ebook)
1. Photography—Printing processes. 2. Albumen paper. I. Title. II.
Title: Albumen and salted paper book.
TR400.R44 2012
773—dc23
                                        2012043695

PREFACE

Silver printing has been often doomed, but it still survives.

—Henry Peach Robinson
& William Abney, Preface to
The Art & Practice of Silver Printing, 1881[1]

———————•———————

The Albumen and Salted Paper Book is a book about the major photographic printing processes in use during the years 1840-1895, approximately the first half-century of photographic history. These first 50 years of photography established a tradition of individual experimentation and craftsmanship in which each photographer (of necessity) participated in the manufacture of the printing materials he or she used. Hardly naive and primitive, the best prints from this era stand as examples of the beauty and subtle tonal perfection that silver photographic prints are capable of, but seldom attain. Yet few people today have any idea of the rich possibilities for contemporary work offered by the fruits of this long tradition of hand-made photographic papers. One important goal of this book is to convey to contemporary photographers an introduction to these traditional methods of silver photographic printing, methods which represent the best that the materials and chemical processes themselves can attain, not what is best for manufacturing economy or darkroom convenience.

The albumen print and the salted paper print were not exotic or eccentric processes in their own time, but were the ordinary, all-purpose materials of photographic printing. The salted paper print dominated photographic practice from 1840 to 1855, and the albumen print did likewise from 1855 to 1895. The albumen print is the second most common type of photograph ever made (though perhaps it has already lost this distinction to the chromogenic color print); it accounts for approximately 85% of the total number of surviving 19th-century photographic prints.

The form of the book is somewhat unusual, in that it combines full working directions for the processes (including quite a few variants of the salted paper print) with extensive historical information about their fabrication and use in the 19th century. It also contains recommendations for the identification, storage and preservation of albumen and salted paper prints, whether they be of historical or contemporary origin. Structuring the book to include more than the working directions for the processes seemed a natural outgrowth of my own interest in the subject, which had always seemed to move by turns from admiring historical photographs and wondering how they were made, to wanting to produce my own images in the same manner. Therefore, I have attempted in the book to preserve the resonances between the historical context and the working directions that made my own practice of the processes so much more rewarding. In time, I also came to be concerned with the factors affecting the permanence of prints made by these processes, and with techniques for their preservation. The central purpose of the book, however, is to offer a contemporary technical account of the making of these 19th-century printing papers, and as a consequence, the treatment of related aspects of the subject (such as identification, etc.) must remain somewhat brief and introductory.

The book is designed to serve the needs of two kinds of readers, those who simply seek technical information on these historical materials, and those who might wish to actually make prints according to these traditional means. At present *both* kinds of readers have nowhere else to look for this kind of information but the original technical writings of the 19th and early 20th centuries. Very good general histories of photography such as those by Newhall and Gernsheim do exist, but these do not provide detailed technical information.

For a modern reader confronting the original 19th-century sources, the difficulties are legion, beginning with the unexpectedly vast extent of the available material. There are also problems arising from variations of terminology and units of measurement, as well as a fairly sizeable amount of contradictory information. Probably the biggest difficulty of all lies in determining how representative of general historical practice any given formula or procedure really is.

To this end one of the main purposes of *The Albumen and Salted Paper Book* is to condense and distill the essence from literally hundreds of original 19th-century writings into one modern, readable account. I have also tried to provide a modern scientific explanation of some of the underlying chemical phenomena, whenever this seemed to help clarify either the history or the practice of albumen and salted paper printing. At the same time I have attempted to convey these technical explanations in as simple and understandable terms as possible.

My greatest hope in writing this book is that more people will experience the kind of pleasure and fulfillment that I have derived from exploring some of the possibilities of these printing papers from photography's past. If they do, they will come, as I have, to respect and understand more fully the achievements of the great masters of 19th-century photography.

I wish to acknowledge here the help and support of some of the people who made this book possible: my wife Linda, who gave the most valuable kind of support; Lionel Suntop and the whole Light Impressions organization; Irving Pobboravsky for his friendship, help and encouragement; and also my colleagues and friends of the Chicago Albumen Works, Joel Snyder, Doug Munson and Gordon Wagner, whose beautiful work in reprinting original negatives on albumen and salted papers would be greatly admired—I am sure—by the original photographers themselves. Also, I am indebted to David Kolody for permission to describe some of his working methods, to Reese V. Jenkins for his guidance and help, to Grant Romer for his advice and counsel, to Volkmar Wentzel for making available some of his father's manuscripts, to Carol Sullivan for her help in manuscript preparation, to Karen Reixach for her editorial work, and finally to Connie Shermer for her efforts in the design, layout and production of this book.

James M. Reilly
Rochester, New York
July 1979

CONTENTS

CHAPTER 1

BASIC PRINCIPLES

There can be no doubt that for purely practical reasons the use of silver printing-out papers has greatly diminished in favor of develop-out papers. Yet printing-out papers will always be valued by those who seek higher image quality in the sense of fine execution and tonality, because in these things some kinds of printing-out papers—and I cite the albumen print as an example—have never been surpassed.

—Fritz Wentzel, 1927[1]

Printing with Silver Salts

The processes described in this book are all based on the fact that salts of silver are light-sensitive—that is, they chemically disso-ciate and form particles of silver metal in the presence of light energy. Silver salts have provided the basis for most photographic materials over the entire course of photographic history. Many other light-sensitive substances are known, and many of them—notably iron, platinum and chromium salts, as well as recently discovered photo-sensitive polymers—serve as the foundation for useful photographic printing materials, but all these systems lack the versatility of silver salts. Used singly or in combination, compounds of silver can pro-duce a great variety of negative and positive images.

There are two large families or evolutionary strains of silver print-ing papers, differentiated by the way in which the image is formed. Most modern photographic papers belong to the class of materials known as develop-out papers, which means that the image is formed by the *chemical* reduction of silver particles after a brief exposure to light. Of course, all practical negative materials have been of the develop-out variety, since the chief advantage of this approach is that only a small amount of light energy is needed to create the image. Less well known is the fact that only since about 1905 have most printing papers been of the develop-out variety.

Printing-Out Papers

For the first 65 years of photographic history the chief method of producing prints was by means of the printing-out processes, wherein the image is formed by the action of light energy alone, without chemical development. Obviously, more light energy is needed than with develop-out materials, in some cases 100,000 times more. Historically, this meant that for printing-out papers daylight was the only practical light source, and even now it remains the cheapest and most satisfactory source in cases where mass production is not required. Printing-out papers are almost unknown today but they are still sold for the purpose of obtaining quick proofs of portrait negatives, though even this application is dwindling as color continues to grow in importance in the photographic industry.

Figure 1.

Checking the progress of exposure. Half of the hinged back of the printing frame is open, while the other half is still closed to maintain registration of the print and the negative.

Printing-out papers possess the advantage that because the image appears during exposure, the progress of exposure may be checked visually and stopped at the right moment. Another advantage of printing-out papers is that they have a very long tonal range, and can successfully reproduce detail from negatives of greater density range than develop-out papers can. In general, negatives that produce good prints on printing-out papers are too contrasty for even the "softest" grades of develop-out papers. The biggest disadvantage of printing-out papers from the modern point of view is their inability to produce prints by enlargement; the amount of light energy required to enlarge onto printing-out papers is enormous and impractical, so all prints must be made by contact.

Classification of Printing-Out Papers

Within the large class of printing-out papers there are two smaller classes or subdivisions—emulsion papers and salted papers. The differences between them come from the way in which the paper is rendered light sensitive, although both kinds depend on the same light sensitive substance, silver chloride. Salted papers are made in a two-step process whereby the "salt" (usually ammonium or sodium chloride) is first applied to the paper and then converted to silver chloride by a treatment with silver nitrate solution. Emulsion papers are made by a one-step process of coating the paper with silver chloride already formed and dispersed in an emulsion. The making and coating of emulsions is best done by machine, although it is possible to produce emulsion papers by hand on a small scale. The salted papers are eminently more practical to produce on a small scale basis, however, and are capable of a widely varied range of effects, textures, colors, and contrasts.

This book is about papers that belong to the category of salted papers, using the term in its technical sense defined above. The term "salted paper" can thus be taken to mean any handmade silver chloride printing-out paper made in two steps, a "salting" step and a sensitizing step. The fact that the two operations of salting and sensitizing are separate allows a much wider choice of materials to be used as a "binder" in which to disperse the silver chloride and keep the image on the surface of the paper. Many materials, most notably albumen, are unsuitable for emulsion-making yet are useful for salted papers. It is necessary here to mention that although albumen paper is a salted paper in the technical sense of the term, most people reserve the term "salted paper" to describe any handmade silver printing-out paper other than albumen paper. This ambiguity has arisen because albumen paper has such towering historical importance that it is usually talked about separately from all other salted papers, though it does actually belong to that class of materials.

Characteristics of Printing-Out Papers

The characteristics of printing-out papers of all kinds differ greatly from those of develop-out materials. The most obvious difference is that of image color. While developed images generally are black (sometimes with a greenish or bluish cast), the color of printing-out papers after fixation is usually yellowish or reddish brown. To most people the color of fixed printing-out papers is not pleasant or agreeable, so a toning process is usually carried out prior to fixing, which alters the color to brown, purplish brown, purple, or black. It is the basic mechanism of image formation in printing-out papers which is responsible for their color. When silver chloride is acted upon by light, it dissociates into its component parts of silver and chlorine, and a tiny particle of metallic silver is formed. These tiny particles form larger aggregate particles that do not exceed a certain size, and which are relatively much smaller than the filaments of silver that are generated in develop-out papers by the action of the developing agent.

The aggregate silver particles that are formed in printing-out papers are of a size that chemists call *colloidal*, which means that they have special properties with respect to light. The particles are not large enough to absorb all wavelengths of light and thus appear black. Instead they absorb some wavelengths but not others, depending in part on the index of refraction of the material in which the particles are dispersed. In practical terms this means two things: first, different binders or vehicles used to carry the image, such as albumen, gelatin, or starch, will produce prints of different colors. Second, when the print is fixed, the color will change dramatically, since by dissolving the unreduced silver chloride present in the light-sensitive coating the index of refraction of the whole system will be changed, and the silver particles will be "packed" together more closely. These are the reasons why prints which have a rich purple or brown color after exposure change to a reddish or yellowish brown in the fixing bath. After drying the prints again change color, becoming darker and colder in tone because the index of refraction of the system and the distances between particles have changed, thus affecting which wavelengths of light are absorbed. The fact that the colloidal silver image changes color depending on the nature of the vehicle or binder material used on the paper constitutes some means of controlling print color, but the toning process plays a greater role and provides more possibilities for control.

Silver Chloride

As stated above, it is light energy alone that reduces the silver salts to metallic silver and thus forms the image in printing-out papers. While many compounds of silver exhibit the print-out property, the most useful for printing papers is silver chloride. Silver chloride is insoluble in water and in most solvents, so it cannot simply be brushed on to make photographic paper. It must be formed in place by a process of first treating the paper with a soluble chloride like sodium chloride—table salt—and then treating it again with a solution of silver nitrate. The two chemicals react, forming silver chloride and sodium nitrate, the latter of which takes no role in forming the image and either dissolves into the silver solution or is washed away in processing.

Pure silver chloride paper is unsatisfactory for printing purposes because it produces gray and flat images. Successful printing with silver chloride depends on the presence of two additional factors: "active" organic substances and excess silver nitrate. Both of these are needed to impart adequate sensitivity and a rich appearance to printing-out papers. It was William Henry Fox Talbot, the inventor of negative-positive photography, who first realized the critical relationship between the relative amounts of chloride and silver nitrate. He found that when chloride and silver nitrate were present in equal amounts his papers were hardly light-sensitive at all, compared to when silver nitrate was present in great excess. Talbot found that about six times more nitrate was necessary and established that the "salting" solution should be 2-4% in strength and the silver nitrate 12%. The reason why so much silver nitrate is necessary was explained by the great 19th-century photochemist Hermann Vogel, who reasoned that as light energy dissociates each unit of silver chloride, the chlorine that is liberated simply unites with the silver nitrate present to form new silver chloride. Light breaks down this newly formed silver chloride, and the cycle begins again, to be repeated over and over. When excess silver nitrate is available, more image silver will be formed and a greater maximum density attained.

The Role of Organic Binders

Experience has shown that certain organic substances have a very favorable effect on image formation in printing-out papers, and these may be designated "active" organic substances. The most important are albumen, gelatin, and organic acids, such as citric, tartaric, and oxalic acid. These "active" organic materials facilitate the more complete reduction of silver chloride and also themselves form light-sensitive substances when in contact with silver nitrate (silver albumenate, silver citrate, etc.). There are many other organic substances used for printing-out papers which are not "active" in the same way, that is, they do not facilitate more complete reduction of silver chloride, but definitely do make a contribution to the printing paper by keeping the light-sensitive materials on the surface and preventing a dull "sunken in" appearance. The most useful of these substances is starch, although lactose, agar-agar, carageenan and resins have also been used for the purpose.

One of the most basic dynamics with any photographic paper is the location of the light-sensitive layer, that is, whether it is confined to the surface of the sheet or has penetrated deeply into the paper fibers. In the latter case the maximum density obtainable on the material will be lowered and the prints will have a matte surface, because the light reflected from the paper will be scattered and diffused by the paper fibers. If the image is produced in a compact layer resting on top of the paper fibers, this scattering is minimized and the maximum density obtainable is much greater. Also, if the light-sensitive coating is itself composed of some smooth and transparent substance like gelatin or albumen, the scattering of light in the white areas of the print will be minimized as well, and the paper will look more "brilliant" and have more contrast. All the various binder materials used in salted papers perform the function of preventing the penetration of the image layer into the paper fibers, although the results also depend on the nature and amount of binder used.

Another benefit of keeping the image on the paper surface is a gain in sharpness and capacity to render fine detail. The early history of printing papers shows a steady evolution of techniques for producing papers capable of greater resolution and contrast, fueled by a desire to reproduce the fine detail present in negatives on waxed paper and glass. Obviously the basic smoothness of the raw paper stock has a great effect on the resultant print, arid so does the amount of organic material coated onto the raw paper. Albumen, for example, may be applied in pure form to produce a glossy paper or may be diluted to any strength, with a corresponding loss of gloss, detail, and "brilliance" of image.

Figure 2.
The would-be photographer
confronts his textbook and
chemicals. From a 1903
advertisement.

Relating Theory to Practice

The terminology and basic theoretical considerations described above are, of course, not enough to carry out the practice of making albumen and salted papers, but they do form a framework in which to begin work. The historical literature abounds with recipes for all sorts of salted papers, including some with very exotic ingredients and procedures. With patience and care, most of them will "work." The difficult part at first is relating theory to practice, and persevering until the true cause of a difficulty becomes evident. Most of the problems that beginning printers encounter are not the result of defective formulae, but of difficulties in coating techniques.

With whatever sort of paper is desired—albumen, arrowroot, etc.—it will be necessary to get a "feel" for the exact method and amount of coating that will produce the best results. Also, coating methods which seem effortless for one person may be totally unworkable for another. For beginners, it is best to trust the formulae as given, and focus on striving for rich, even coatings. Do not be afraid to try out new ideas for coating methods. Once a "feel" for the basic materials and coating methods is established, it is then possible to create variations on formulae and fulfill the promise of creative expression with a totally unique photographic material.

The key to success in every operation described in this book is clean and careful work. Because of the presence of excess silver nitrate, the printing-out papers are far more subject to damage from careless handling and contamination than are modern photographic papers. Contamination is a very real danger, and only good housekeeping practices will prevent it. Failure to clean up spills will load the air in work areas with chemical dust, and uncleaned trays will surely cause stains in prints. A thorough and careful approach to housekeeping in work areas is actually part of a whole attitude that leads to good results. This attitude is one of patience and care, and a thoughtful attention to detail. Success will come through a process of slow refinement of results and not through discovering the one "right" formula. A system of record keeping is essential, both to obtain repeatable results and to understand the causes of problems.

Any work with the methods described in this book will help to make a direct link with a photographic tradition from which "convenience products" in photographic materials have made us very distant. Respect and understanding for the achievements of early photographers cannot help but grow from acquaintance with their methods.

CHAPTER 2

WORKING ENVIRONMENT EQUIPMENT AND MATERIALS

The printer should be allowed everything of the best quality to work with, and have a comfortable room to work in.

—Edward L. Wilson, 1881[1]

Work Areas

The best approach to organizing work areas is to follow the plan adopted by 19th-century portrait galleries—to have two separate working rooms, a "wet" fabrication area and a "dry" printing area in which to load printing frames and store equipment away from chemical contamination. It is preferable but not absolutely necessary that these two areas be separate rooms, but if they must share the same room, rigorous cleanliness is required. Certain requirements are common to both areas. Ideally, they should both be well lit, well ventilated, and maintained at 18-20°C and 45% relative humidity. The capacity to eliminate white light from all work areas is also necessary. Both areas need safelight illumination; for this purpose yellow "bug-lite" 60-watt incandescent bulbs work perfectly. There is no need to work in the dim light of safelights required for modern papers. The level of illumination should be bright enough to see and work comfortably. In the 19th century, windows of printing rooms were simply hung with yellow curtains or painted over with yellow paint.

The "Wet" Area

The primary purpose of this area is to provide a place for the coating, drying, and processing of materials. The operations involved in coating and sensitizing should be carried on in an area that can tolerate the possibility of spills and stains. Drippings from papers hung up to dry are inevitable, and somehow silver nitrate stains always appear on floors and tables despite all precautions. A basement room is a very practical choice, providing it can be kept clean and humidity can be controlled. The level of cleanliness certainly does not have to be that of industrial paper coating facilities, but ought to be as clean as any well-kept darkroom.

Generous counter space should be available, and also adequate storage for chemicals, trays, glassware, and other equipment. Although a darkroom sink is not necessary, a sink of some kind is necessary and a darkroom type is helpful. There should also an area where freshly coated papers may be hung to dry. For safety reasons, sensitized papers should not be hung where people may pass underneath them. The floor underneath this section may be covered with plastic or newspaper to catch dripping. Ordinary clotheslines and plastic clothespins (papers tend to stick to wooden ones) serve well, and the lines should be strung at an angle of 5 to 7 degrees in order to concentrate runoff at one corner of the sheet. It is sometimes helpful to accelerate drying of papers with heat; if the room is small, portable electric heaters will serve the purpose. *Always* check to make sure that electrical wiring is adequate to handle the load created by portable hearers. Each 1250-watt heater should be placed on a separate circuit and heaters should never be left unattended.

THE "DRY" AREA OR PRINTING ROOM

Once the printing papers have been sensitized and dried the actual operations of printing may begin, and for this purpose an area is needed that is free from the danger of splashing chemicals and airborne contamination. Counter space is required, and storage for printing frames when not in use. Daylight should be excluded from the printing room altogether, but incandescent white lights and yellow "bug-lite" safelights are necessary. It is difficult to evaluate the progress of exposure under yellow light; white lights may be turned on long enough to make the inspection. Incandescent white light is preferable to fluorescent light for inspection purposes because the chances of fogging the paper are lessened. Two drawers, one for unexposed paper and the other for exposed prints, are also helpful. If conditions of temperature and relative humidity are appropriate, then negatives may be conveniently stored in the printing room as well. The printing room may also double as a print finishing area, since this operation, too, must be kept away from chemical contamination.

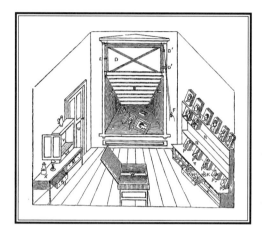

Figure 3.

A printing room, ca. 1875. Printing frames are being exposed in a window shelf. An ammonia fuming box is shown at left.

Equipment

Items of necessary equipment will include the following:

LABORATORY BALANCE

It is necessary to weigh out amounts of chemicals with reasonable accuracy, but a sophisticated and expensive laboratory balance is not required. A "student" grade balance with a capacity of 2000 g and an accuracy to 0.5 g will be satisfactory. A two-pan type of balance is inexpensive and convenient. Note that throughout this book the symbol g is used to mean the metric *gram*, a unit of weight equal to 15.432 *grains*.

Figure 4.

A typical laboratory balance of the 1880's.

MEASURING AND MIXING CONTAINERS

For most purposes of measuring and mixing, polyethylene gradu-ated beakers with handles are the most practical. They are unbreak-able and easily cleaned. A 1000 ml and a 2500 ml model should be enough for most mixing needs. For measuring small amounts of liquids a 100 ml cylinder graduate with 1 ml graduations will be helpful. A generous supply of glass or plastic stirring rods is also necessary. A three gallon plastic or porcelain pail will come in handy if large amounts of liquids are to be mixed, and the pail may double as a dishpan for cleaning laboratory glassware. Trays and glassware should be cleaned with Alconox™ or Sparkleen™, detergents spe-cially made for cleaning laboratory articles.

TRAYS

Trays that have been in use for ordinary photographic procedures are usually unsatisfactory for albumen and salted paper printing be-cause of contamination. A good approach is to buy new trays and to label them for each operation, so that there is one tray reserved for sensitizing, toning, and fixing, respectively. Porcelain trays are preferable, as long as they are not chipped in any way. Very inexpen-sive porcelain trays may be purchased from restaurant supply stores. While they may not be in the usual photographic formats—8 x 10, 11 x 14, etc.,—they are still serviceable, and far cheaper than trays sold for exclusively photographic use. The tray reserved for the sil-ver solution is especially susceptible to chemical contamination, and ideally should be made of glass. If glass is not available, then a new porcelain or plastic tray will do.

Figure 5.

Glass trays, although breakable, were easily kept clean and free of contamination. From a 1901 advertisement.

WHITE PORCELAIN
GLASS TRAYS.

For Plates.	Price.
4 x 5	$0.20
5 x 8	.30
7 x 9	.50
8 x 10	.60

PRINTING FRAMES

The printing frame is perhaps the single most important piece of equipment used in albumen and salted paper printing. The purpose of the printing frame is to provide a means of keeping the negative in direct contact with the paper during exposure, and at the same time allow the paper to be inspected and returned to contact in exact register with the negative. The basic design of printing frames has not changed very much since the 1840's; it consists of a wooden frame with a pane of glass in front, and a hinged back that fits in-

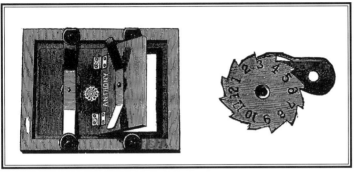

Figure 6.
"Anthony's Improved Printing Frame". A closeup view of the counter device is shown at right.

side the frame and is held in place by springs. The reason for the hinged, two-part back is so that one spring may be loosened, half of the back opened, and the progress of the exposure checked while the still-closed section holds the negative and print together to maintain registration. A felt or chamois pad is used between the paper and the back of the printing frame to evenly distribute the pressure and insure good contact over the entire print area. The use of such pads was very common in the 19th-century, but so little contact printing is done today that most people are unaware of their benefits. When printing from 8x10 or larger film negatives, pads are indispensable, especially with the poor quality printing frames available at the present time.

Printing frames should be at least one "format" larger than the negative in use—a 5x7 frame for a 4x5 negative, for example,—and they should be kept clean and dust-free. They should be of sturdy construction, with double-thickness "picture glass," not ordinary window glass, and have a good-quality laminated back for strength. Sadly, the printing frames available from photographic dealers today fall far short of those made in years past that were intended for rugged professional use. Many currently-made frames have backs of aptly-named "chipboard," which will constantly release wood splinters and spoil prints and negatives unless the utmost care is taken. It is still possible to find older printing frames made of beautifully finished hardwoods at antique stores or flea markets, or even from dealers in antique photographica, but the larger sizes of these are scarce. The older frames are a joy to use and are often less costly than their painted plywood descendants.

Many older frames have a counter device on the back. This can take the form of a notched wheel with incised numbers or may be a pointer arm that points at embossed numbers; the purpose of these counters was to keep track of the number of prints made from a given negative. With many frames and negatives in use at one time it was a handy accounting system for the quantity of prints made from each negative.

Paper

Paper suitable for albumen and salted paper printing must be of the highest standards of purity. Only papers which are "all-rag"—meaning that they are formed of pure cellulose—are acceptable. Prior to the 1920's the only way to produce a pure cellulose paper was to make it from cotton or linen rags, since the fibers of these plants are composed of cellulose in a pure form. Papers made from other plant materials, such as wood pulp, straw, or hemp, contained impurities that reacted with chemicals in sensitized coatings and speedily led to the destruction of the image. Even in the ab-

Figure 7.
Cutting rags for papermaking. Better grades of paper were made from selected rags hand cut into small squares on a special inclined knife.

sence of a sensitized coating, impurities in such papers eventually converted to acids, which would cause yellowing and brittleness. The science of papermaking at the present time does allow wood pulp to be purified until mostly pure cellulose remains, and papers are now produced for photographic purposes which have no cotton or linen content, yet are equal to true "rag" papers in nearly every respect. Another reason why "all-rag" papers are necessary is their great strength, especially when wet; ordinary paper would simply fall to pieces if subjected to the rigors of coating, sensitizing, and processing. Even lightweight rag papers—which are preferable because they are easier to manipulate in floating steps—will not tear in processing.

In addition to the composition of the fibers, other criteria for paper selection are the color and texture of the surface. Coarse-textured, porous surfaces will tend to absorb the light-sensitive coatings, and the resultant prints may be flat and dull. If prints look better by transmitted light than by reflected light, then the solutions have sunk too deeply into the paper fibers, and either a pre-sizing step or more viscous coating is needed. If paper is tinted, the color should not be too strong and in any case should harmonize with the color of the photographic image. Paper with a smooth surface and white color is a good starting point from which to become acquainted with the color and textural qualities of various light-sensitive coatings and toning techniques.

Smooth-surfaced papers are the result of a combination of heavy sizing (sizing is the material added to the paper pulp to bind the fibers together and create a smooth surface on the sheet) and rolling between rollers to further flatten and polish the surface. If a very glossy print is desired, the paper should be as smooth as possible to begin with. Matte paper may be generated either by coating a smooth sheet with a matte coating material like starch, or by coating a porous sheet with a relatively more viscous and smooth coating.

In the 19th century, obtaining the proper paper for albumen and salted paper printing was a very difficult problem, especially for the large-scale production of albumen paper. Two firms emerged in the 1850's as producers of reliable paper for photographic use2 and dominated the world market until 1914, when the press of wartime need forced the development of new production facilities. These two mills, one in Rives, France, near Grenoble and the other in Malmedy, Belgium, supplied nearly all of the photographic rawstock consumed in the 19th century. They possessed the natural advantage of being located on mineral-free water supplies, which, together with their experience in the specialized needs of photographic paper, ensured their continued success.

Binder Materials Used in Printing Papers

Many organic materials—proteins mainly but also some carbohydrates—are useful as binders or vehicles in which to disperse silver chloride and at the same time confine it to the print surface. Albumen, gelatin, starches, and whey were all in use for salted papers before 1855. Of these, albumen was by far the one most widely used in the 19th century. It is also the only one of the binders that an experienced eye may identify with reasonable certainty with just a cursory examination of a print. The following short descriptions of binder materials does not constitute an exhaustive list, and it touches only on those properties of the materials which bear on their photographic use.

ALBUMEN

Albumen for photographic purposes may be taken to mean the clear white of a hen's egg. Actually many specific proteins can be identified in egg white, but when used collectively they are referred to as albumen. Albumen has a specific gravity of 1.040, and at room temperature it dries to a brittle, transparent mass. Albumen may currently be obtained as a powder, of which a 15% solution in water will approximate native egg white, but the powdered albumen is more costly and less convenient for photographic use than albumen obtained directly from eggs.

Albumen is insoluble in alcohol, and in fact alcohol will coagulate albumen, a property that is useful to obtain multiple coatings of albumen on a single sheet. Albumen is also coagulated by temperatures above 65°C and by contact with salts of metals. The reason why albumen does not dissolve off the sheet during processing is because contact with silver nitrate in the sensitizing bath coagulates it and forms a new insoluble silver-albumen complex called silver albumenate. This substance itself is light sensitive and makes an important contribution to image formation in albumen paper.

The pH of native egg white is 7.8. Albumen is used in this fresh alkaline condition only for matte papers, and for these it is always mixed with starch or other substances. Glossy papers are prepared with partially decomposed acidic albumen, because in that condition it creates a glossier surface and more even coating, and has less tendency to yellow after sensitization. Albumen is never used in the strictly native condition; before any photographic use may be contemplated, the egg whites must be beaten to a froth and allowed to settle back to a liquid state. This beating process denatures the various proteins—all of which have different viscosities—and results in a homogeneous liquid which will form an even layer on the sheet of paper.

Figure 8.
The leghorn chicken,
displaying an ideal
shape for maximum
egg production.

GELATIN

Like albumen, gelatin is not a specific substance but a collection of proteins. Gelatin is obtained by cooking the skins, tendons, and bones of cattle in a pH controlled vat of water. If the temperature and pH of the cooking liquor are carefully controlled, very pure forms of gelatin may be obtained. In cold water, dried gelatin swells to a viscous mass, which will melt at temperatures above 32°C. Gelatin is not precipitated by metal salts in the same way that albumen is, but additions of alum to solutions of gelatin result in gels that are harder and less permeable. Adding potassium chrome alum results in gels that are completely insoluble. Formaldehyde also exerts a hardening effect on gelatin.

Gelatin lends a characteristic reddish color to salted paper prints. The first salted papers made by Fox Talbot showed this reddish color, not because Talbot had included gelatin in his "salting" solution, but because the gelatin was already present on the paper, put there as a sizing by the paper manufacturer.

STARCHES

Starch occurs widely in the plant kingdom, and exists as microscopic white grains that are insoluble in alcohol, ether, and cold water.

When starch is heated in water, the grains burst and a turbid paste is created. The turbidity and adhesive properties of starch pastes vary with the origin of the grains. Although many different kinds of starch may be used for photographic purposes, certain ones are preferred because the pastes they produce are pure white, very viscous, odorless, and of low turbidity. Among these the most important is arrowroot, which comes from the West Indian plant *maranta arundinacea*, though tapioca and sago are also useful. When starch pastes are applied to paper and dried, a layer is formed that will not swell in water and will withstand the processing solutions without damage. Starches do not react with silver salts and have no effect on the reduction of silver chloride. Most salted papers that use starch as a binder will therefore also have an "active" organic substance—usually citric acid—as part of the formula.

RESINS

Resins are noncrystallizable, amorphous substances which are obtained from plants, notably the sap of softwoods such as pine and fir. Resins are distinguished from gums by their insolubility in water. They are soluble in alcohol, ether, etc., and such solutions are known as lacquers. When mixed with alkalies such as ammonia or sodium hydroxide, they form foamy solutions known as resin soaps; if acids are added to resin soaps, the resin is precipitated in an insoluble form. Resin soaps are also precipitated by contact with silver nitrate solutions, forming an insoluble white mass that is moderately light-sensitive.[3] The presence of resins has no effect on the reduction of silver chloride.

CHAPTER 3

SALTED PAPERS

A print on plain paper may be dead, foggy, inky, sunk in the paper, &c., &c., but in its most unhappy state it does not look vulgar; there is always a certain sentiment about it, even in its worst phase of failure.

—Thomas Sutton, 1856[1]

Photographic Printing Before 1850

Although others before him had experimented with the light-sensitive properties of silver chloride, it was the Englishman William Henry Fox Talbot who prepared the first successful silver chloride photographic paper. This discovery came in the years 1834-1835,[2] and laid the foundation for all the subsequent printing-out papers that were so extensively used in the 19th and early 20th centuries. The details of Talbot's method were not revealed until 1839,[3] after news of Daguerre's success had spread around the world. Talbot's "photogenic drawing" paper was prepared in two steps: first, fine quality writing paper was immersed in a weak salt solution and dried. The second step involved making the paper light sensitive by brushing on a strong solution of silver nitrate. The sensitized paper darkened when placed in sunlight, and was "stabilized" against further darkening (at low light levels) by washing the paper in a strong salt solution.

At the suggestion of Herschel, Talbot changed to sodium thiosulfate, or "hypo" as the fixing material, and this made the prints completely stable to light and left them with white highlights, instead of the pale lilac highlights characteristic of fixation in strong saline solutions. With the adoption in 1839 of "hypo" as the preferred method of fixation, Talbot's "photogenic drawing" paper had evolved into what is now known as "plain salted paper", the positive printing

Figure 9.
A facsimile of a photogenic
drawing that appeared in
The Magazine of Science
for April 27, 1839.

material that was to become almost universally used during the decade 1840-1850. During that time plain salted paper was commonly referred to as "ordinary photographic paper", to distinguish it from various types of develop-out papers.

Talbot had tried to use his "photogenic drawing" paper in the camera to make negatives, but exposures were so long that he abandoned print-out negatives as soon as a practical alternative was available. He retained the print-out method for positives, however, because the results were more controllable and in his eyes more aesthetically pleasing. He thus set the pattern for the whole 19th century; development was regarded as a necessary evil for negatives, and as too troublesome and unpredictable for positives. Also, the greenish-black color of developed positives was widely reviled as "inartistic."

Although he himself employed only a plain salt solution as the first step in making the paper, Talbot's prints were reddish brown in color and reflected the presence of gelatin, used by the paper manufacturer as a sizing material. French photographers found that the papers they used did not produce the same results as English papers did, because starch sizing was used by the French paper-makers instead of gelatin. Until the late 1840's no organic binder materials were used in the salting solutions for salted papers, only chlorides—usually table salt or sea salt. Photographers were at first quite puzzled by the different results from English and French papers, but eventually two French scientists, Alphonse Davanne and Jules Girard, investigated and explained the phenomenon.[4]

———————•———————

Plain Salted Paper

Plain salted papers are those which have little or no organic binder material, and are thus matte-surfaced and of relatively lower maximum density. However, for even a simple salted paper, some organic material is necessary; it must either be present in the paper before the salting solution is applied, or it must be added to the salting solution itself. In practice, it is usually more convenient and satisfactory to add organic material to the salting solution. The sizing that already exists in papers is usually insufficient, and without additional organic binder material the resultant prints would appear too flat.

A salted paper which closely approximates the printing materials of the 1840's can be made as follows:

SODIUM CHLORIDE	20 g
GELATIN	2 g
WATER	TO MAKE 1 liter

Swell the gelatin in 250 ml of cold water, then heat the rest of the water and in it dissolve the sodium chloride. Mix the hot water and gelatin together, and when it has cooled to approximately 80°F, it is ready to use. The paper is salted by floating it on the salting solution for three minutes. This solution contains far less gelatin than modern gelatin emulsion papers; the amount of gelatin is only enough to slightly inhibit the sinking of the image into the paper fibers. Hence the choice of rawstock for this or any other plain salted paper that does not contain very much viscous binder is extremely important and has a great influence on the results. Porous rawstocks such as watercolor paper will yield very flat prints indeed; early photographers generally chose the smoothest rawstocks available to them, and for plain salted papers that are not made with viscous binders it is best to imitate their choice of a fairly smooth paper.

A variant on the above formula for plain salted paper is:

SODIUM CHLORIDE	20 g
SODIUM CITRATE	20 g
GELATIN	2 g
WATER	TO MAKE 1 liter

The addition of a neutral citrate will cause the prints to be more reddish in color and slightly more "brilliant." However, the porosity of the rawstock will still be the largest single factor in the resultant prints. Both of these simple salted papers will require the same sensitizing, toning, and fixing. Detailed descriptions of these operations will be found in later chapters.

With whatever paper stock has been chosen, examine the paper closely before salting it to see if there is a difference between sides--usually there is a front side and a back side, meaning that one side is smoother and has more sizing than the other. The front side is the smoother one, and that is the side that should be coated with the salting solution. If there is a watermark visible, then the front is facing up when the watermark is readable. Once the paper has been salted and dried, there will be no way to tell which side has been treated, so it is necessary to mark the back of each sheet in pencil--to keep track of which side has been salted.

FLOATING THE PAPER ON THE SALTING SOLUTION
Floating is the preferred method for coating most salted papers, because it eliminates the possibility of patches of uneven density which might be caused if both sides are "salted." These patches of uneven density result when some of the silver solution is drawn to the back of the sheet during sensitization, thus locally sensitizing some areas on the back and causing a blotchy appearance on the face of the print.

With some rawstocks, however, the simple gelatin salting solutions given above will provide good results when the paper is immersed and not floated. Only experience will determine which rawstocks can be successfully salted with the immersion technique.

The technique of floating is not difficult, and it actually becomes quite efficient and routine if the proper conditions are maintained. If the temperature of the paper itself and the salting solution is the same, the floating of the paper is made considerably easier. If the salting solution is warmer than the room temperature—which is also the paper temperature—then the sheets of paper will curl ferociously when they are placed upon the surface of the solution. In general, relatively thin papers are preferable because they are easier to handle, especially after they have been coated with binder materials and must be floated a second time on the sensitizing bath. Paper becomes stiffer when dry, and so a certain amount of moisture in the storage environment of the paper, especially just prior to floating, makes the sheets easier to handle.

Curling is caused by the swelling of the paper fibers on the bottom of the sheet, so if curling does occur it can be remedied by dampening the fibers on the top side of the sheet. Old manuals recommend breathing on the sheets to unbend them after they have curled, but this is impractical for all but the mildest curling.

After a sheet has rested on the surface of the solution for awhile, it will uncurl itself and gradually lie flat. But if the curling has been too severe, the sheet may be already ruined from the solution running on to the back. Sometimes holding the edges of the sheet down

Figure 10.
Salting paper by immersion.

on the surface of the solution until the sheet uncurls itself is a workable method, but with large sheets this may take two people. With whatever method is chosen, it is always best to try to have conditions of moisture and temperature as favorable as possible before attempting to float. One way to control curling is by dampening the back of the sheet with a fine mist of water after it is placed on the solution. The inexpensive plastic atomizers sold for various garden uses will work well, but large droplets of water must not be allowed to collect on the back of the sheet while it is floating, and only a minimum of dampening should be used. An alternative approach, which works well for some people, is to fold back about ½ inch of paper on all four sides of the sheet, thus making a kind of "boat". The creased edges resist the tendency to curl and the folded flaps help prevent the solution from reaching the back of the sheet.

Many old manuals advise that paper be floated by handling it by two diagonal corners, bending the sheet and placing the center of the bent sheet on the surface of the solution. It is then gently lowered until the corners touch down and the sheet floats on the surface. This technique nearly always results in a line of bubbles becoming trapped under the sheet in a diagonal line from the two corners not held in the hands.

A better way is to first fold over about ¼ inch of paper in two opposite corners of the sheet, so that these two bent corners act as little handles to give better control of the sheet. Grasping the paper by these two bent corners, bow the sheet and place one corner of it on the solution. Gently lower the other hand until the whole sheet

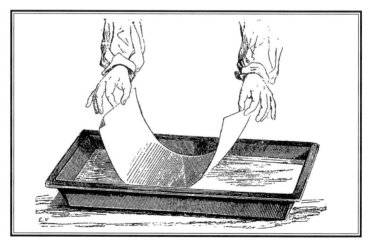

Figure 11.
Salting paper by floating it
on the salting solution.

THE ALBUMEN & SALTED PAPER BOOK

rests on the solution. The advantage of this approach is that the bubbles that may have formed when the sheet first touched down on the surface are forced out to the edges by the rolling motion from one corner to the other, instead of from the middle to the two corners at once as the old manuals suggest.

If any bubbles do appear, lift the sheet from one corner and if they do not break of their own accord, pierce them with a toothpick and replace the sheet on the surface. Bubbles may usually be seen through the paper itself, but if the stock is too thick, then the sheets will have to be lifted from the corners to check for bubbles. Time the operation of floating from the point at which all bubbles have been broken and the sheet rests evenly upon the surface.

When the sheets have floated for the required length of time, carefully lift one corner and slowly raise the sheet from the solution. The sheets will be coated more evenly if they are slowly peeled from the surface. By slowly lifting them there will be less dripping of liquid back into the tray of solution, and fewer bubbles will be formed in the tray to interfere with the next sheet to be floated. Always check the surface of the solution for dirt or bubbles before attempting to float a sheet of paper.

The sheets should be hung to dry by the two corners of the long edge, so that the downward runoff has the least distance to travel. This minimizes the unevenness of Coating which always occurs because the solution runs downward toward the floor, forming a slightly thicker coating on the lower half of the paper. If the sheets curl during drying, clothespins may be clipped to the bottom edge of the sheets to weight them down. Heat may be used to accelerate drying, but with plain salted papers there is no advantage gained except faster drying.

When the sheets are dry, they should be taken down and pressed flat under some weights. This makes them more supple and easier to handle in the sensitizing step. The paper will keep indefinitely in this salted condition, if stored in a cool and dry location. Of course all salting operations may be conducted in white light, since the paper is not light sensitive until it has been sensitized on the silver nitrate solution.

Paper made according to the above two formulae should be sensitized by floating for 3 minutes on a 12% silver nitrate solution. After the paper is sensitized, however, it will keep for only one or two days, depending on the temperature and humidity of the storage environment.

CONTRAST CONTROL IN SALTED PAPERS

Each type of silver printing paper has a characteristic gradation and contrast. This means that only a certain type of negative will give the optimum results with each kind of salted paper. For example, the plain salted papers given above are very soft-working papers and require negatives of far greater density range than any modern develop-out paper. The reasons for this have to do with the basic nature of printing-out papers and the smoothness or porosity of the paper stock. A detailed explanation of the tone reproduction characteristics of albumen and salted papers will be given in Chapter 7, but briefly stated, the more matte-surfaced a paper is, the lower the contrast of that material is likely to be. Albumen paper, therefore, requires a less contrasty negative than plain salted papers.

Techniques for increasing the contrast of printing-out papers do exist, and they can be especially useful in printing negatives with a less than optimum density range. In the 1840's the paper negative processes then in use were well suited to salted paper printing, since they often produced "harsh" negatives. For modern negatives that have been made for printing processes with greater inherent contrast, it is helpful to have a means by which such negatives may be printed on salted paper. Controlling the intensity and color of the exposing light is one convenient way to control contrast, and this is discussed more fully in Chapter 7. The chloride content of the "salting" solution also has an effect on contrast.[5] Large increases of contrast are possible only with the use of chromates, and this technique does allow otherwise unprintable negatives to produce good prints. Nevertheless, the judgment of years of experience by many different writers on silver printing is that the best salted paper prints are always made in sunlight with optimum negatives, and without resorting to contrast enhancing additions to the salting solution.

The addition of chromium salts to the salting solution is the basic method of contrast enhancement. This technique is presented here only as an alternative for use when a print is desired from a too "thin" negative; it has no place in regular practice, since the finest results may only be obtained by using the "pure" processes with optimum negatives.

The discovery that chromium salts led to higher contrast was made by Ferdinand Hrdliczka in the mid-1890's—a time when printing-out papers were gradually losing ground to the developing-out papers.[6] For most of the 19th century, photographers depended mainly on control of the negative density for contrast control in the print; that is why so many intensifier formulae are found in 19th-century photographic manuals. Chromated papers were introduced to the market in the late 1890's, but their sales amounted to only a small portion of the total sales of printing-out papers.

Potassium bichromate is the chromium salt most often employed for the purpose of increasing contrast. A convenient way to use it is to make a 5% stock solution with distilled water. **CAUTION! Potassium bichromate is a toxic substance and should be handled with care.** Some individuals are extremely sensitive to it, and all contact with the skin should be avoided. Wear eye protection and gloves, and avoid inhalation of dust by wearing a disposable surgical mask when mixing the bichromate solution. Always work in a well ventilated area.

The bichromate stock solution is added to the salting solution in varying amounts depending on the degree of contrast enhancement desired. The effect of bichromate additions is mainly on the highlight areas of the image.

A sample salting solution containing bichromate is:

SODIUM CHLORIDE	25 g
5% SOLUTION POTASSIUM BICHROMATE	5 ml
GELATIN	2 g
WATER	TO MAKE 1 liter

Sensitize for 3 minutes on a 10% silver bath which also contains 5% citric acid.

It is best to keep bichromate additions to a minimum. The stability and predictability of papers declines with increasing amounts of bichromate. The practical limits of contrast control with this technique will have to be established through experience. In no case should the dry weight of bichromate exceed 1% of the salting solution. The disadvantages of bichromate additions include the toxicity of the substance, the fact that papers must be salted and stored in yellow or diffused white light because of the light sensitivity of potassium bichromate itself, and the necessity of avoiding any contact of the salting solution with metals, since these react unfavorably with bichromates. Also, the addition of bichromates tends to produce a browner image color than would otherwise be obtained. Bichromate additions will serve the same contrast-enhancing function in almost any kind of printing-out paper, and they are employed in approximately the same quantity with other papers as with the plain salted paper formula given above.

Arrowroot Papers

Arrowroot paper is a form of salted paper in which the binder material is a paste made from boiled arrowroot starch. The surface qualities of arrowroot paper range from very matte to a dull gloss, depending on the amount of starch applied to the paper and the smoothness of the underlying rawstock. Arrowroot prints can be considerably more brilliant and richer-looking than plain salted papers; they have a longer density range and preserve more delicate detail.

The first starch papers were prepared by DeBrébisson in 1854[7] using tapioca instead of arrowroot, but eventually arrowroot emerged as the most suitable and widely used starch for the purpose. Starch papers became very popular and almost completely displaced plain salted papers for matte-surfaced prints. In 1854, the popularity of albumen paper was increasing as well, but a significant number of photographers still preferred a matte surface on their prints. At that time, albumen paper was very new and had its share of problems— it was harder to tone and fix than other kinds of paper, and it was sometimes difficult to coat evenly and the newly discovered starch papers represented a great advance over the older plain salted papers. The middle 1850's saw the rise of a new kind of business enterprise offering salted and sized photographic papers to the public as an article of trade—and many of the new companies sold both albumen and starch papers.

However, significant improvements in albumen paper were not long in coming, and during the last half of the 1850's albumen paper ascended to the unchallenged dominance of the photographic paper market that it was to keep for the next 35 years. Although diminished in popularity after 1860, starch papers continued to be used by a small number of photographers, and arrowroot paper remained an article of commerce well into the 20th century. Unfortunately, starch papers appeared at a time when the public taste was very much on the side of glossy papers, which were a novelty at the time and better suited to the small but immensely popular *cartes de visite* size portraits. In a typical full-length pose, the head of a person in a *carte de visite* might be less than ½ inch high, so maximum detail was necessary in the print to make such a tiny image successful.

After 30 years, public taste began to change again, and glossy papers fell out of favor. In the 1880's the first awakening of a renewed interest in matte papers was felt, led by photographers whose main interest in photography was aesthetic, not commercial. By 1900, the public at large had come to regard matte papers as more "artistic," and although there were a great number of printing methods to satisfy the demand, arrowroot papers enjoyed a modest revival along with plain salted papers. The application of platinum toning methods allowed a whole range of brown tones to be produced, and this helped increase public acceptance of arrowroot papers. The poor economics of professional portraiture with expensive and time-consuming printing-out papers eventually drove the last arrowroot and plain salted papers off the market in the years following World War I.

PREPARATION OF ARROWROOT PAPER

Arrowroot prints can be made on almost any sort of paper surface, but a fairly smooth surfaced paper is generally preferred. Highly calendered "plate" finish papers present a little more difficulty in obtaining an even coating. Arrowroot pastes tend to be absorbed into the paper fibers—in fact, they must be absorbed to a certain extent to adhere—and so porous papers will require a binder that contains a higher percentage of starch.

The salting solution is prepared as follows: rub 35 g of arrowroot into a creamy paste with a little cold water. This is best done in a mortar and pestle. Add enough cold water to make a fairly runny "cream" with no lumps. This "cream" will tend to separate into its components, so it must be stirred or rubbed up to the moment of use. Separately dissolve 35 g of sodium chloride and 3 g of citric acid in 950 ml of water. This solution should be brought to a boil in a porcelain container, and the arrowroot cream added in small amounts with constant stirring using a glass rod or wooden spoon. Allow the mixture to gently boil for a few minutes and then remove from the heat. When the mixture has cooled it is ready to use. Remove the skin that forms on the surface of the cooled liquid; this is the residue of the hulls of the burst grains of starch. Tapioca or rice starch may also be used in the same manner as arrowroot.

The formula for arrowroot paper is essentially the same as for plain salted paper except that it contains citric acid. Starch is not an "active" organic substance and so has no effect on the reduction of silver chloride. Hence if the citric acid which is "active" were not present, the prints would be gray and flat, and hallmarks of a pure chloride image. In the presence of both citric acid and starch the prints take on a warm purple color after exposure, and, in the absence of toning, change to a yellowish-brown after fixation.

COATING OF PAPERS WITH
ARROWROOT SALTING SOLUTION

There are many approaches to applying the starch salting solution to the paper. Always mark the back of the sheet in pencil before applying the salting solution. Salting solutions that contain 2% arrowroot or less are fluid enough to allow the paper to be floated on the starch solution. This is a little more difficult than floating paper on albumen or thin gelatin solutions, and will not provide as much binder on the surface of the paper as other methods. Heavier coatings of starch may be obtained by immersing the sheets in the salting solution and drawing them out over a glass rod, or between two glass rods held tightly together.

The method most recommended in old manuals is first to pin the sheet of paper to a flat board, and use a thin flat brush to apply a 3-4% starch paste. The salting solution is lightly applied by brushing first in one direction, and then distributed with perpendicular cross-strokes. The paste is allowed to sink in for a minute or two, then a round dry brush is used to even out the coating and remove excess paste until a uniform matte surface is obtained. The difficult part is to keep the coating as even as possible at every step of the operation. If the paper is textured, care must be taken to Ensure that the paste is uniformly brushed into all the crevices. Still another approach is to apply the paste with a sponge, wait 1 or 2 minutes, and scrape off the excess with a squeegee, first in one direction, then the other. The paper is hung to dry after it has been coated with the salting paste. Only experience will determine which is the best approach to coating the paper for any given paper stock or individual.

Arrowroot paper should be sensitized by floating on a 12% silver nitrate solution that also contains 4-5% citric acid. The length of time for floating starch papers on the silver bath is generally shorter than with other papers. If the coating of arrowroot is not a heavy one, then ½ minute may be sufficient. For heavily coated papers, 1 ½ minutes at most may be required. Too long floating on the silver bath results in gray and flat prints, especially with porous papers. The silver nitrate solution may also be applied with a wide brush. Citric acid additions to the silver bath will produce paper that will keep several weeks after sensitization. The toning of arrowroot papers may be done with any of the toning formulae given in Chapter 8.

Resume of Processing Steps for
Albumen and Salted Papers

The individual operations in the processing sequence of salted papers—toning, fixing, washing, and drying—are dealt with in depth in separate chapters. For the sake of clarity, a brief overview of all the processing steps for a typical albumen or salted paper print is as follows:

STEP 1: INITIAL WASH
In order for the papers to have the necessary sensitivity, they must contain an excess of silver nitrate (see Chapter 1). The initial wash—usually about 10 minutes in running water—is the first step in processing and it serves to remove this excess silver nitrate. If it were not removed at this stage, the silver nitrate would retard or completely prevent any toning from taking place, and if it were still present when the print is fixed, black stains would be the result. In large-scale printing operations the first wash water is carefully saved, and from it the majority of the silver used to sensitize the paper is recovered.

STEP 2: TONING
The toning process is the largest single factor in determining the final color of the print. It is performed before the fixing step—although it may be done after fixing with equal success—because the toning process forms silver chloride as a by-product, and this would therefore resensitize the print if it had already been fixed. The toning step is performed in weak white light if the prints are to be toned by inspection and not "by rule." Otherwise all the processing steps up to and including the fixing are performed in yellow light.

STEP 3: WASH BEFORE FIXING
A short wash—3 to 5 minutes in running water—is given before the prints are transferred to the fixing solution. Interaction between the fixer and toner may cause changes in the fixing solution that would damage the color and permanence of the prints.

STEP 4: FIXING
The purpose of fixing is to remove the unreduced silver chloride and other light-sensitive substances such as silver citrate, etc., which may

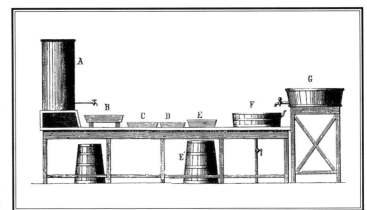

Figure 12.
A processing line for
albumen prints. Trays B &
C are for the initial wash;
D is the toning tray, and E
is the fixer tray. F and G
are for washing the prints.

be present. A fixer composed of an alkaline 15% solution of sodium thiosulfate solution is useful for all albumen and salted papers. The time of fixing should be 8 to 10 minutes. For maximum permanence, two fixing baths are used. The prints should be fixed for 4 minutes in each bath, and drained for at least 5 seconds before being placed in the second fixing bath. A fresh batch of fixer should be made for each printing session; the extra silver present in salted papers quickly exhausts fixing baths, and even unused fixer solutions break down very rapidly.

STEP 5: WASH BEFORE HYPO CLEARING TREATMENT
The prints should be given a short (2 to 4 minutes) wash in running water before treatment with a hypo clearing agent. This wash removes a large portion of the hypo and avoids overloading the mechanism of hypo removal.

STEP 6: TREATMENT WITH A HYPO CLEARING AGENT
The use of a hypo clearing agent is recommended to aid in the more complete removal of silver-thiosulfate complexes which may cause damage to the print. A 3-to 4-minute treatment in 1% sodium sulfite solution is required.

STEP 7: FINAL WASH
Depending on the thickness of the rawstock, the prints should receive at least a 30-minute wash in an effective print washer. Heavier weight papers may require longer washing.

STEP 8: DRYING

Prints may be dried in a number of ways. A good approach is to gently blot them on high quality photographic blotters and air dry them face up on fiberglass screens.

CHAPTER 4

ALBUMEN PAPER

I believe the albumen print will be the print of the future, as it is that of the present. It is for the present and coming photographers to make its future better and more enduring than its past.

—W.H. Sherman, 1892[1]

The Early History of Albumen Paper

The first published notice of the use of albumenized paper in photography occurred in the following letter, which appeared in *The Athenaeum*, May 11, 1839:

> *Photogenic Drawing*—Considering that any (however trifling) improvement will not be unacceptable to those of your readers who feel an interest in this art, I have been induced to communicate the following method of preparing the paper, which, after many experiments, I find to succeed best. Wash the paper with a mixture of equal parts of the WHITE OF EGG and *water*, afterwards with the solution of nitrate of silver, fixing the drawing as usual with the iodide of potassium. H.L.[2]

To the as yet unidentified experimenter "H.L." must go the honor of having produced the first photographs on albumen paper. It is notable that his or her work with albumen followed so closely upon Talbot's revelation on Feb. 21, 1839, of the actual working details of "photogenic drawing" (plain salted paper).

Of course, the method described by "H.L." differs from the usual practice of the albumen printing process in one vital respect: it does not call for the addition of any chlorides to the albumen, and therefore depends solely on the light sensitivity of "silver albumenate." Not until 1850 did Blanquart-Evrard supply the missing chlorides and earn the distinction of having invented the albumen printing process in its most practical and useful form (see below).

Although "H.L." was the first person to make albumen paper without chlorides, he or she was not the last. The very first general treatise on photography, Robert Hunt's *Popular Treatise on the Art of Photography* (published in Glasgow in 1841), includes this suggestion:

> By soaking the paper in a solution of isinglass or parchment size, or rubbing it over with the white of egg, and drying it prior to the application of the sensitive wash, it will be found to blacken much more readily...[3]

Probably very few photographers made albumen prints by this method, since the results with plain salted paper were far superior. The idea of using albumen without chlorides was "rediscovered" in 1865 by Schultner[4] and actually proposed as a practical and economical printing method in 1866 by Schnauss.[5] Albumen prints made without chlorides required a weaker than usual silver solution and a fairly contrasty negative, but the resultant prints have surprising vigor and tone well in gold toners. However, the use of chlorides produces a far more versatile and satisfactory printing paper, and in 19th-century practice chlorides were always used.

INVENTION OF THE ALBUMEN PRINTING PROCESS

The albumen printing process as it was actually used during the 19th century was the invention of Louis Désiré Blanquart-Evrard, a pioneer French photographer who made many important contributions to photography. He was both a talented photographer and a technical innovator, and his writings on photography were very influential. Without doubt his most useful and far-reaching discovery was the albumen print, the photographic medium upon which the last half of the 19th century was recorded.

The discovery of albumen paper came in the late 1840's as Blanquart-Evrard searched for improvements in Talbot's calotype process. Blanquart-Evrard tried and was somewhat successful in using albumen as a carrier for the light-sensitive salts on paper negatives, and he went further and adapted it to the usual method of making positives on plain salted paper. It worked splendidly as a positive material, and provided a deeper, bolder image than could be obtained on the matte salted papers of the day.

Blanquart-Evrard communicated his discovery to the world in a brief account of his various photographic researches which he presented to the French Academy of Sciences on May 27, 1850.[6] Photographers were quick to try out the new method for positive prints, and it became an almost instant success. By 1855 most serious photographers had at least tried—if not adopted—albumen paper.

Blanquart-Evrard's original recipe for the preparation of albumen paper was simple; white of egg was beaten to a froth with 25% by weight of a saturated salt solution, and the mixture was allowed to settle overnight. The solution was then placed in a tray and the paper was floated on the albumen for one minute and hung up to dry. The dried paper was not light sensitive and would keep indefinitely in the albumenized condition.

To print with the material, the paper had to be sensitized by floating on a strong solution of silver nitrate and dried again. It was then ready to place in the printing frame and expose to daylight. Thus, it may be seen that albumen paper is essentially the same process as plain salted paper, except that egg white is employed as a binder material to close the pores of the paper and retain the light sensitive substances in a compact layer on the surface. It is precisely because the image is retained on the print surface that albumen paper represented such a great advance in print boldness and contrast, and that it possessed increased capacity to reproduce fine detail.

The albumen printing process appeared at almost the same time as the discovery of the revolutionary wet collodion negative process by Frederick Scott Archer. These two photographic materials were seemingly created to meet the needs of each other; tonally, albumen paper made fine prints from the kind of negatives that the wet collodion process generated, and the increased capacity for detail in the albumen print exactly answered the needs of the new glass negative. By 1860 they had become established as the dominant and almost the only negative and positive materials used in ordinary photographic practice, and they remained so for the next 20 years. Around 1880 the gelatin dry plate began to replace the wet collodion negative, but the albumen print remained the most popular printing material until 1895. At that time emulsion-type gelatin and collodion printing-out papers captured the market and ended the 40-year dominance of albumen paper.

Albumen paper changed considerably over the years between its introduction in 1850 and its ultimate disappearance as a commercial article in 1929.[7] The earliest albumen prints strongly resembled the salted paper prints of the late 1840's; they were chocolate brown or reddish brown in color, but of course did possess some degree of added gloss and depth, depending on the amount of water added to the albumen. Two great technical advances in the albumen printing process that solidified its primacy were the introduction of alkaline gold toning methods and the refinement of coating techniques to allow for quite glossy prints. Both of these refinements were made in the decade 1850-1860.

Improved toning baths made possible not only a wider range of image colors, but also significantly increased the durability and resistance to fading of the prints. The man responsible for this fundamental advance was James Waterhouse, who first applied alkaline toning sometime around 1855. More detailed information on the history of toning can be found in Chapter 8.

The other important advance was not the product of any one person but represented an evolutionary process based on experience, as photographers strove to make the process of coating albumen simpler and more effective. The great *desideratum* of the period was the attainment of greater gloss and detail, and it was found by many experimenters working independently that partially decomposed—in chemical terms "denatured"—albumen yielded a glossier and more even coating. Decomposed albumen passes into an acid condition and forms a homogeneous mixture without the uneven viscosity and stringiness of native egg white. Some albumenizers went so far as to actually allow the albumen to naturally ferment at elevated temperatures for several days. The origins of the fermentation technique are uncertain, but fermented albumen was already in use by the mid-1850's as a substratum on glass plates to improve the adhesion of collodion.[8] This technique later became standard procedure in the Dresden, Germany, factories, which from the early 1870's on supplied the majority of the world's albumen paper. Not surprisingly, Dresden paper could readily be identified by the smell.

It also became apparent during the 1850's that albumen paper required a certain type of raw paper stock in order to obtain the best results. Experience showed that a thin, smooth paper of exceptionally high quality was necessary for success. The production of such paper was no easy matter; the main difficulties were the prevention of metal flecks in the paper and the need for an abundant supply of mineral-free water. These kinds of impurities proved extremely troublesome both in the paper manufacturing process and also when the paper was coated with highly reactive photographic solutions. The causes of metal flecks in the rawstock were metal buttons left in the rags used to make the paper, and bits of metal breaking off the paper-making machinery itself. Since water purification techniques were not very advanced at that time, only nature could provide a supply of mineral-free water, and such places were rare. The mill of the Blanchet Frères et Kléber Co. in Rives, France, was located in a valley and used water from a nearby mountain lake, fed by "the melting of the alpine snows."[9] Apart from all this was the enormous amount of capital required to construct a paper mill, and the fact that the skill and experience of the staff above all else contributed to a *consistently* good paper.

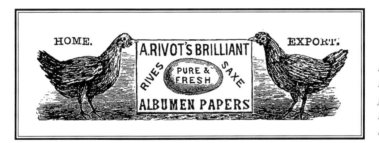

Figure 13.
1885 advertisement
for albumen paper.
Note references to "Rives"
and "Saxe" rawstock.

It is no wonder that only two paper mills in the world managed to consistently produce a paper of the necessary quality, and these two mills were able to maintain their monopoly from the 1860's until approximately World War I.[10] They were the above-mentioned Blanchet Frères et Klébler Co. in Rives, France (hence their product was known as the "Rives" paper) and Steinbach and Company, located in Malmedy, Belgium (at that time part of Germany). Steinbach paper was known outside Germany as "Saxe" paper. Both papers were machine-made all-rag papers, sized with a mixture of starch and resin soap. One analysis of Rives photographic rawstock conducted in 1904 showed it to be comprised of 85% linen fiber and 15% cotton fiber.[11]

In the late 1850's and especially after 1860, two new factors in photographic technology and practice generated a great demand for albumen paper. The first of these was the stereograph; its ability to transport the viewer to distant scenes with the illusion of three-dimensional reality depended largely on the smooth surface and fine detail of albumen paper. Stereo views were extremely popular, and created a corresponding demand for albumen paper. Nearly all stereo views before 1890 were made on albumen paper.

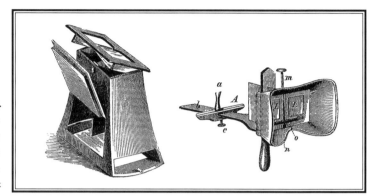

The other factor was the emergence of cheap portraiture for the masses in the small format known as *carte de visite*, or the visiting card photograph, called by the public simply "card pictures." These consisted of an albumen print on a cardboard mount that was approximately 6 x 10 cm in size. The *carte de visite* mania originated in Paris and soon proved to be the greatest stimulus for the photographic gallery trade since the daguerreotype, and the cheap and

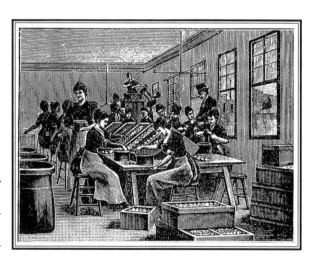

Figure 15.

Manufacture of albumen paper in Dresden, Ca. 1890. The first step is to separate the eggs.

THE ALBUMEN & SALTED PAPER BOOK

easily multiplied portraits were popular in all strata of society. Famous people, great works of art, advertising material, faraway places and patriotic tableaux all were reproduced on *cartes de visite* and eagerly collected and traded by the public. The photograph album soon became a ubiquitous household article, and all this fueled the demand for albumen paper.

To be sure, the possibilities of albumen paper as an article of commerce attracted enterprising photographers, and as early as 1854 albumenized paper appeared for sale in Germany.[12] Many small companies in Western Europe undertook to produce albumen paper, but for various reasons Germany emerged as the center of world production by the year 1870. In the United States during the 1850's the tendency was to import rawstock from Europe for individual photographers to albumenize themselves, but during the Civil War a change took place, and from then on most photographers bought the paper already factory-coated with albumen. American photographers could choose among four major American brands or from an assortment of German products.[13] American and English producers were at the immediate disadvantage of having to import the rawstock from France and Germany, where the paper mills which produced it were located. In the United States the centers for albumen paper manufacturing were Philadelphia, Rochester and New York. After 1880 the importance of the German producers grew, and they took control of an even larger share of the American market than they had enjoyed in the 1870's. In 1890 the editors of *Anthony's Pho-*

Figure 16.

Two types of stereo viewers. Most stereo views produced during the 19th century were made on albumen paper.

tographic Bulletin complained loudly about an increase in the tariff on albumen paper, declaring that American photographers use German paper "in a proportion of four to one of domestic paper, and this in spite of its higher price on the market."[14]

Figure 17.
The albumen is then fermented in large casks for several days.

The city of Dresden, Germany, became the center of the burgeoning albumen paper industry. Close to the sources of rawstock and enjoying an abundant supply of low-cost eggs, Dresden also had the advantage of lower labor costs than English or American competitors.[15] As a result, Dresden soon had enough manufacturing experience to add consistent high quality to its list of advantages. As mentioned

Figure 18.
Paper is then floated on the albumen solution and hung on racks to dry.

above, the Dresden firms used naturally occurring bacteria in the albumen to initiate a fermentation process that lasted several days. The fermented albumen provided glossier paper that toned more easily. However, other European and American producers made good quality albumen paper using aged but not actually fermented albumen.

Figure 19.
The coated paper is "calendered" in rolling presses to make it more flexible.

Some idea of the scale of the Dresden production may be gained by considering that one company (there were two major ones and several smaller ones in the city), called the Dresdener Albuminfab-riken A.G., in 1888 produced 18,674 reams of albumen paper.[16] Each ream consisted of 480 sheets 46 x 58 cm in size. To coat a ream of paper required 9 liters of albumen solution, obtained from 27 dozen eggs. Thus total production for that one year in this one factory consumed over six million eggs. As may be seen in the accompanying illustrations, the procedures in the manufacture of albumen paper are manual ones, and it is really a handicraft product, quite different from the machine-made photographic articles of the present day. Each sheet of albumen paper was floated by hand, and in some cases floated twice on the albumen in order to obtain a glossier coating. The illustrations show that nearly all the tasks in albumen paper factories were performed by women, and this was the case in both European and American factories.

A very large percentage of the albumen paper produced during the period 1870-1900 was tinted various shades of pink, purple and blue by adding aniline dyes to the albumen before coating it on the rawstock. The first such paper appeared on the market in 1863[17] and

attained great popularity in the 1870's and 1880's. Tinted paper was mainly used for portraits, and of all the myriad shades produced, pinks seem to have been the most popular. Because the dyes used had poor stability to light—especially in such diluted form—most of the dyed paper is difficult to recognize today. In some cases although nothing remains of the original tint of the paper, a peculiar buff or chamois cast identifies albumen prints that were originally made on tinted paper. This "dirty" color was noticed in the 1890's and the use of tinted paper advised against for that reason.[18]

Until the mid-1890's albumen paper reigned supreme as the workhorse photographic printing material, meeting the needs of very diverse users with equal facility. The state of printing and photomechanical reproduction in the last half of the 19th century did not provide for an easy and cheap way to reproduce photographic images, so actual photographic prints—albumen prints—were used for many advertising, educational and utilitarian purposes. Albumen paper was so pervasive in the last third of the 19th century that the phrase "silver print" was understood by everyone to mean "albumen print."

Preparation of the Albumen Solution

The first step in the production of albumen paper is to prepare the albumen solution itself. Only the freshest available eggs should be used, even though the albumen will be allowed to age before coating it on the paper. Each large egg will provide about one ounce of albumen. The difference between eggs produced in assembly line fashion in massive henneries and eggs laid by well fed, free-running chickens is quite considerable. Although the latter sort are preferable, supermarket eggs will suffice for the purpose of preparing albumen paper. The eggs should be separated completely and only the clear white saved—without the slightest contamination of yolk, blood or the stringy tissue known as the chalazae. Small, inexpensive egg separators are available at housewares outlets and are a convenient way to separate eggs. A good plan is to separate the eggs over a small bowl and pour the albumen into a larger bowl after each egg is separated. This way, if some contamination occurs, it is not necessary to attempt to remove a small amount of contaminant from a large amount of albumen.

In the 19th century the yolks were preserved with salt and sold to bakeries or to tanners, who used them to finish kid leathers. The money realized from the sale of egg yolks was a large factor in the profit and loss statements of the giant Dresden albumen paper producers.[19] When the number of yolks is not on the industrial scale, the *British Journal of Photography* for Sep. 2, 1861 (p.313), provided this recipe:

A HINT TO ALBUMENIZERS—What can you do with the yolks of your eggs? Make them into cheesecakes that will be pronounced unrivalled. Dissolve a quarter of a pound of butter in a basin placed on the hob, stir in a quarter pound of pounded lump sugar, and beat well together; then add the yolks of three eggs that have previously been well beaten; beat up all together thoroughly; throw in half of a grated nutmeg and a pinch of salt, stir, and lastly add the juice of two fine-flavored lemons and the rind of one lemon that has been peeled very thin; beat up all together, thoroughly, and pour into a dish lined with puff-paste, and bake for about twenty minutes. This is one of the pleasantest "bye-products" we are acquainted with in the economics of manufacturing photography. Try it!

When the albumen has been obtained from the eggs, the next step is to beat it to a froth with the appropriate amount of ammonium or sodium chloride. Prints with similar color and contrast may be expected with the use of either of these chlorides, or both used in combination in the correct amount. The amount of chloride used has a definite relation to the sensitivity, and to a small extent, the contrast of the paper. Papers with a low (1-1.5%) chloride content are less sensitive and tend to produce slightly more contrasty prints from thin negatives than do papers with the normal chloride content of 1.5-2.5%. This slight gain in contrast is at the expense of a rich, dense image, however, so it is best in ordinary circumstances to keep the chloride at 1.5% or above. On the other hand, the use of more chloride in the formula than is necessary only results in higher silver consumption without conferring any additional benefit. The chloride—ammonium chloride was the most commonly used in the 19th century—should be dissolved in a minimum of water and added to the egg white before the beating process. If a blender is used to beat the egg whites it is not necessary to dissolve the chloride in water.

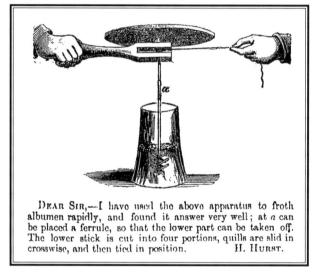

Figure 21.

H. Hurst's submission to The Photographic News for Nov. 12, 1858, expressing his ideas on the subject of frothing albumen.

DEAR SIR,—I have used the above apparatus to froth albumen rapidly, and found it answer very well; at a can be placed a ferrule, so that the lower part can be taken off. The lower stick is cut into four portions, quills are slid in crosswise, and then tied in position.   H. HURST.

Dear Sir,—I have used the above apparatus to froth albumen rapidly, and found it answer very well; at a can be placed a ferrule, so that the lower part can be taken off. The lower stick is cut into four portions, quills are slid in crosswise, and then tied in position. H. Hurst.

Beating the albumen is necessary to accomplish the task of chemically breaking down the different protein substances until a more or less uniform substance is created. While beating to a froth does the major work of evening out the viscosity of albumen's different components, further "denaturation" by chemical means must take place before the albumen is ready to apply to the paper. The chlorides added are vital to the formation of the photographic image, but they also help to denature the albumen; one of the effects of adding chlorides is to reduce the volume of froth produced during the beating step. The third kind of denaturing treatment usually employed is the adjustment of pH by the addition of acids or alcohol. The chemical forces which bind together the enormous molecules of protein grow weaker as the pH is lowered, and the physical properties of the substance change as a result. The effect of adding chlorides and acids, such as acetic acid, and finally beating the egg white is to completely and irreversibly change it. After settling for 24 hours and aging in a refrigerator for one week it is a yellowish homogeneous liquid with a slight "aged" odor that signals its readiness for use.

A sample preparation of albumen might be as follows:

AMMONIUM CHLORIDE	15 g	
GLACIAL ACETIC ACID	2 ml	combine and add to:
WATER	30 ml	
ALBUMEN	1 liter	

The mixture should be beaten in an electric mixer or blender for 3 minutes, or until the entire mixture has been converted to a froth.

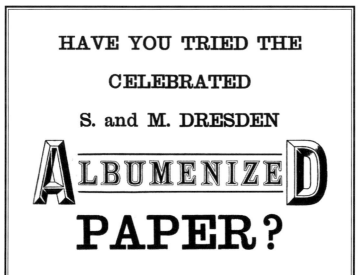

Figure 22.
An 1874 advertisement for Dresden paper in an American photographic book, The Practical Printer.

Allow the mixture to settle in a covered container for 24 hours. Strain the mixture through muslin; the liquid may have to be squeezed through the muslin with some pressure. Cover and refrigerate for one week. The albumen solution will remain useful for several weeks after the one-week aging period. The smell of the albumen and its color, sedimentation, etc., will reveal when it has decomposed too badly to use.

Coating Paper with Albumen

The basic mechanism of coating consists of filling a tray to a depth of approximately ⅔ to ¾ inch with the albumen solution and floating the paper on the surface for 1½ minutes. The choice of paper for albumenizing is somewhat limited, since paper of the type commonly used for the purpose in the 19th century is not readily available in art supply stores. A thin, smooth all-rag stock is necessary, and perhaps the closest approximation of the ideal that

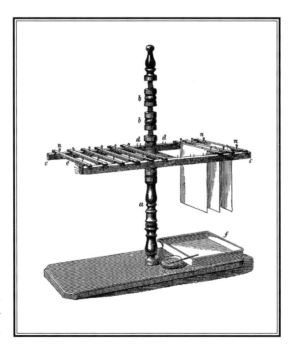

Figure 23.

A drying rack for albumen papers.

is available in most areas is Strathmore Series 500 drawing paper, one-ply, with the plate finish. Although it is somewhat heavier than the usual 19th-century rawstocks, this paper will perform satisfactorily.

To coat the paper, first condition both the paper and the albumen solution by allowing them to gradually come to the operating temperature of the work room. When ready to coat, filter the albumen through muslin and place it in a tray slightly bigger than the size of sheet to be coated. Immediately before a batch of paper is to be floated, it is helpful to add a surfactant such as Kodak Photo-Flo™ 1:200 to the albumen solution. Use 4 ml of Kodak Photo-Flo™ for each liter of albumen, and gently stir it into the solution, avoiding bubbles as much as possible. The purpose of the surfactant is two-fold: first, it controls bubbles—one of the most troublesome aspects of the whole process—and second, it improves the runoff characteristics of the albumen during drying and promotes a more even coating. The commonly used jargon for surfactants in photographic coating plants is to call them "spreaders," which graphically sums up their benefits in the coating process.

The actual procedures and precautions of the floating process itself are the same as those described in Chapter 3 for plain salted papers. Albumen paper must be coated on one side only and cannot be immersed in the solution. With thin papers air bubbles trapped under the sheet will be visible as light circles on a dark background, and if they appear, the sheet must be lifted by one corner and the bubbles broken. With thicker paper the bubbles will not be visible through the sheet, so each sheet must be lifted off the surface and the bottom side inspected for bubbles. Floating paper requires a little skill, but it is not really difficult and experience is the best teacher. It is best to start with a sheet about 10 x 12 inches in size, since this leaves plenty of margin area when one 8 x 10 or four 4 x 5 prints are desired. The time of floating should be 1 to 1 ½ minutes. Time the process from the moment all bubbles are broken and the sheet lies flat on the surface of the solution. Lift the sheet slowly off the solution and hang it to dry by two corners along the long edge of the sheet.

The arrangements necessary for drying the sheets are the same as those for plain salted papers described in Chapter 3. One additional factor is present with albumen paper, however, and that is the effect of heat on the drying process. The higher the temperature of the drying environment, the faster will be the drying, and more importantly, the glossier will be the paper. Temperatures of 30 to 50°C were maintained in drying rooms in albumen paper factories in the 19th century. High temperature drying is not necessary, but it does offer a way to improve the gloss and depth of single-coated albumen papers. During the process of drying the albumen will collect along the bottom edge of the sheet. If this runoff is allowed to dry, a thick rind of albumen will form and make the sheets very difficult to work with in subsequent operations. In addition, the last droplet will take a very long time to dry. The remedy for this is to blot off the collected runoff with a cloth several times during the drying process. The sheets should dry in a relatively short time if this precaution is observed. When dry, the sheets should be placed in a pile and flattened under weights. This makes them supple and easy to handle in the further floating operations to come.

DOUBLE COATING OF ALBUMEN PAPER

There will always be a slight difference in gloss and thickness of coating between the top half of the sheets and the bottom half because of the action of gravity in hanging the sheets to dry. The severity of this effect depends on a large number of factors, but it is usually not so pronounced as to render a batch of paper completely unsuitable for use. Obviously many of the characteristics of the finished prints depend on the thickness and glossiness of the coating of albumen; among these are the ultimate color of the prints, their brilliance and "depth," and the ease of toning and fixing. Toning and fixing are more difficult with thicker coatings because the albumen becomes increasingly less permeable as the coating thickness increases. As mentioned above, one of the most attractive features of albumen paper in the 19th century was its glossy surface and added "depth," so experiments were made to increase the coating thickness by using multiple coatings of albumen. It was soon learned that some form of hardening or coagulating step was necessary between coatings to render the first coating insoluble. Otherwise there was no gain in thickness or amount of albumen on the sheet, because the second coating step dissolved off the albumen remaining from the first coating operation.

There are three possible approaches to hardening the albumen between the first and second coating operations. The simplest and most widely used method in the 19th century was to store the paper in a warm loft for six months, during which time a slow curing process sufficiently hardened the albumen. If a speedier result is desired, there are two "instantaneous" approaches.[20] One is to subject the albumen to a current of steam, which in effect cooks the albumen and renders it insoluble. The other is easier and more practical; it involves briefly immersing the sheets in a 70% solution of isopropyl alcohol. Pure alcohol is too strong and unevenly coagulates the albumen layer, while too dilute alcohol solutions are not strong enough to coagulate the albumen before it partially dissolves into the water. Experience has shown that a 70% solution is the most effective. To prevent leaching out of the chlorides from the albumen, whatever chloride content is present in the albumen itself should also be added to the alcohol solution—if the albumen contains 2% ammonium chloride, so should the alcohol solution.

A satisfactory procedure to accomplish the hardening is simply to place the alcohol solution in a tray and slowly pull the sheets of albumenized paper through the solution and hang them up to dry. When they are dry they should be placed in a pile and flattened under some weights to make them easier to manipulate during the second floating operation.

Mark the edge of each sheet that was lowest when the sheets were hung to dry the first time. This marked edge will be hung as the top after the second floating on the albumen, in order to even out the coating and thereby compensate for the runoff effect.

Two coatings of albumen produce papers that are quite glossy and may even be so heavily coated that they are brittle and hard to tone. Double-coated paper usually produces better prints from thin negatives than single-coated paper does. For more information on this point, see Chapter 7. A large portion of the albumen paper sold after 1880 was of the double-coated variety. However, double-coated papers have a greater tendency to curl, and are harder to manipulate in sensitization and printing.

Sensitizing Albumen Paper

Once the sheets have been albumenized, they will keep very well if stored in a cool and dry place. If the sheets must be rolled for storage, it is better to roll them with the albumen side out so that the cracking of the albumen is minimized. To sensitize the sheets for printing they must not be excessively dry at the time of sensitization, because if too dry, they will not properly absorb the silver nitrate solution. A good plan is to place the sheets overnight in a damp location such as a basement, etc. This also tends to make the sheets more supple and easier to handle. Albumen paper should be floated on a 10-12% silver nitrate solution for 2½ to 3 minutes. No additives to the sensitizing bath are required in the ordinary course of printing. See Chapter 6 for complete information on the sensitization process and the management of the silver bath.

Of course, care must be taken during sensitization to make sure that no air bubbles are trapped under the sheet; bubbles prevent sensitization where they occur, and will cause white circles on the face of the finished print. The sheets must be very slowly and carefully lifted off the silver solution, since no silver solution should reach the back of the sheet, and also because if lifted too quickly, the runoff of sensitizer might cause uneven sensitization. Some old manuals recommend drawing the sheets over a glass rod as they are lifted free of the solution, but this is unnecessary if the sheets are *slowly* peeled from the surface. Mild heat may be used to accelerate the drying of the paper after sensitization, but the paper must not be allowed to become excessively dry at the time of printing. As is the case during the albumenizing steps, the silver solution which runs off the sheets when they are hung to dry must be blotted with blotting paper or a cloth. Not only does this speed the drying process, but it insures more even sensitization.

Ammonia Fuming

One of the most confusing things about researching the albumen printing process in 19th-century sources is the question of ammonia fuming. This was a procedure in which the sensitized and dried sheets of albumen paper were hung in a closed box and subjected to the vapors of ammonia. The ammonia fumes were supplied by placing strong ammonia in a dish in the bottom of the box. "Fuming" was usually carried on for 5 to 10 minutes. The purpose of fuming was to make the paper more sensitive and to obtain richer, more brilliant prints. While it is true that in some circumstances ammonia fuming will produce more sensitive and contrasty paper than would otherwise be obtained, nevertheless ammonia fuming is not necessary in order to produce good results.

The confusion about the practice of fuming arises because ammonia fuming was a quite common practice in the United States and yet was hardly practiced at all in Europe;[21] in Germany the practice was used very infrequently. Reading an American manual, one

Figure 24.

An advertisement for albumen paper, 1894. The tint of the paper and its quality level is shown on the label.

might find the fuming technique given a prominent place, while in a German manual it is only briefly mentioned. The resolution of this apparent contradiction lies in the fact that much of the value of fuming may be realized by simply increasing the strength of the silver bath or by aiming for negatives of slightly different density range. That is, other factors in the printing process may compensate for the lack of fuming and equally good results obtained.

The value of fuming was most important when a paper of low chloride content was sensitized on a relatively weak sensitizing bath. In this circumstance the extra sensitivity conferred by fuming might make a considerable difference in the results. However, with the use of a stronger silver bath only slightly more silver would be consumed, yet the paper would probably be as sensitive as the fumed sheet. In those places where the use of fuming had become customary, other factors in the process adjusted to that custom, and gradually fuming came to be perceived as a necessity; in areas where the practice never became customary, it was reserved for occasional use when extra sensitivity was called for. For the modern practice of albumen printing, the troublesome and unpleasant process of ammonia fuming seems unnecessary.

Printing and Processing Albumen Paper

Albumen paper sensitized as described above will remain in good condition for 24 to 48 hours, depending on environmental conditions. For optimum results it should be both exposed and processed during that period. Care and patience should be exercised in every step of the printing operation, beginning with the loading of the printing frames. Make sure that the glass is clean and that the frame is working properly before risking a valuable negative. If a glass negative is used, a piece of foreign matter such as a splinter of wood between the glass of the frame and the negative can fracture the negative once pressure is applied. Always use felt pads in the printing frames to distribute the pressure, and make sure that the pads lie flat when re-closing the frames after checking the progress of exposure.

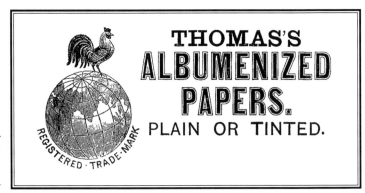

Figure 25.

Chickens and eggs were familiar motifs in albumen paper advertisements.

White light must be excluded from all operations in sensitizing and subsequent handling of the paper, although it is helpful to evaluate the progress of exposure briefly with a low wattage white incandescent light. Yellow light does not allow the separation of tones in the middletone and shadow areas to be clearly seen, and under- or overexposed prints may be the result. The conduct of the printing operation itself is governed by the nature of the negative to be printed. A complete discussion of the factors involved in print exposure may be found in Chapter 7, but in general thin negatives are exposed to weaker and more attenuated light, while dense negatives may require the intensity of full sunlight. Only experience can provide the knowledge of how far to carry the exposure of any given print, but in all cases the print should appear too dark—to a greater or lesser degree—when leaving the printing frame. All prints bleach to a certain extent in the toning and fixing operations, but the exact degree of overprinting necessary will vary for different negatives and batches of paper, and also depends on taste. However, albumen prints require slightly less overprinting than salted paper prints do, and double-coated albumen papers need less overprinting than single-coated sheets.

The color of the prints after exposure will vary from a rich purple to a dark brown. The prints are very beautiful as they come from the frame, and many writers on the albumen printing process have remarked that they wished the prints could be preserved in that state forever. The exposed prints should be kept in a light-tight drawer or box until all prints are ready to be processed. The general outline of processing is the same as that given for plain salted papers at the end of Chapter 3. The first step in processing is an initial wash to remove the bulk of the free silver nitrate. Although the washing should be continued past the point where the wash water is free of the cloudy precipitate of silver chloride, do not allow the first wash to go on past 10 minutes in running water. Excessive washing removes the last small traces of silver nitrate that are necessary for some toners to work properly. The prints should be agitated or other steps taken to see that they are uniformly washed; they are now ready for toning.

Toning Albumen Paper

The main difference between the processing of plain salted papers and that of albumen paper is the strength of the toning bath; albumen prints need a much stronger and more effective toning solution than salted papers do, because albumen is less permeable and the silver particles are more protected. This also means that the toning of albumen prints is usually slower—even with a stronger toning solution--than the toning of salted paper prints. Any variations in the thickness of the albumen coating, especially in the case of double-coated papers, will be immediately apparent in the toning step, because less heavily coated areas will tone more quickly and deeply.

Any of the gold toning baths given in Chapter 8 may be used with albumen paper. They should be used full strength for ordinary glossy albumen paper. A good way for beginning printers to get a sense of the toning process is to leave one print completely untoned, and fix it and dry it with the rest. In this manner a basis of comparison is established for the amount of toning that has taken place.

The historical practice of toning glossy albumen paper involved the used of gold toners almost exclusively, while salted papers and the later matte-albumen papers were toned with either gold or platinum toners or both used in combination. For glossy albumen paper, however, there can be little question of which toning method was usually applied, for all but a negligible few experimental prints were toned with gold toners of the kind described in Chapter 8. Black tones (instead of the usual cool browns and purples) were attainable with gold toners on albumen paper, but never gained great popularity.

The toning step is the focal point of the whole processing operation. Every other aspect of processing may be done "by rule" and is fairly routine, but toning of albumen prints is usually done by inspection. The problem with toning by inspection is that the prints alter dramatically in fixing and drying, and end up a little darker and colder in tone than they appear in the toning bath. Thus is it easy to under- or overestimate the amount of toning that has taken place. The progress of toning, even more so than the progress of exposure, cannot be accurately gauged in yellow light, so a weak white incandescent light is needed at intervals for evaluation of the toning operation. If the light is not too bright it may be left on during the whole toning process, because after the first wash the prints are considerably less sensitive. Another difficulty in toning is that all prints do not tone at the same rate, so that when one print in a batch is judged to be toned, the others in the same batch may not necessarily be toned to the same degree. The necessity of giving the prints individual attention limits the number of prints that may be toned at any one time.

The prints must be kept uniformly wetted and be constantly agitated during toning, or uneven toning will be the result. The gold toning solution should not be made too strong (in order to work more quickly), because too rapid a deposition of gold will spoil the prints. The gold layer will then be merely superficial, and will be largely removed in the fixing bath, leaving a flat and meager looking print. Also, if toning is carried to extremes in a normal strength bath, too much gold is substituted for silver and the prints turn an unpleasant slate blue color, and lose density. There must be a harmonious distribution of both gold and silver in the print to form an image of good color and contrast. Ideally the toning operation should last 10 to 15 minutes or even longer; in this way there is less chance of over-toning, and there is time to consider whether the prints are toned to the desired extent.

In large 19th-century galleries and mass-production printing establishments the toning of prints was a specialized occupation. The "toners" in such places often used their own secret formulas, and each had his or her own special way of determining when a print was correctly toned. One thing to consider that may help in this determination is the extent to which the prints already have a purplish or cool brown color before the toning process is begun. Sometimes prints are quite reddish in color by the time they are ready to tone, and at other times the prints may retain the purplish color at that point. The purple color will completely disappear in the fixing solution, so if the purple color has fooled the "toner" into thinking that the toning has advanced farther than it actually has, then under-toned prints are sure to result. Many old manuals advise "redding up" the prints by placing them in a 3% acetic acid solution for 10 minutes and washing them in running water before attempting to tone them. In the usual course of modern practice, "redding up" will not be necessary, because prints are usually not purplish at the point of toning unless ammonia fuming has been used.

In most cases the prints should take on a definite lilac or purplish tinge during toning, but the process should not be carried so far that the prints look at all bluish. The degree of toning to strive for is a matter of taste, but severe under-toning may lower the expected life-span of a print. The prints may be examined by transmitted light during toning to give a more accurate idea of how much toning has been accomplished. When by transmitted light the last traces of warm color have disappeared from the print, the toning process is quite advanced, and the final color of the print is likely to be purple or purplish-black. Many old manuals advise to tone until the warm color has *almost* disappeared by transmitted light. With each of the gold toning baths given in Chapter 8 there will be slight differences in rate of toning, and with the thiocyanate toner a difference in the mechanism of toning, but the general instructions given above apply no matter which toner formula is selected. When the toning is completed the prints should be given a running water wash for at least 5 minutes in accordance with the general outline of processing given at the end of Chapter 3.

Fixation, Washing and Drying of Albumen Paper

Fixing of albumen prints is done in an alkaline 15% solution of sodium thiosulfate (also called "hypo"). While fixing the prints may appear to be a routine matter that does not require careful attention, in reality the permanence of the prints depends to a great extent on the observance of proper fixing procedure. The object of

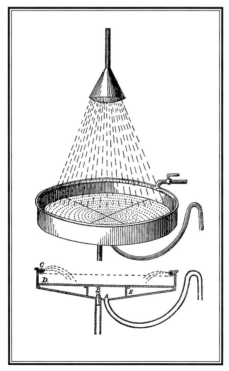

Figure 26.
A novel print washer
suggested in **Photographic**
Mosaics *for 1878.*

fixation is to render the image stable by removing any light-sensitive substances, leaving behind an image of metallic silver. As a practical matter, both fixation and washing of albumen prints is made more difficult by the nature of albumen itself, since coagulated albumen is resistant to penetration by solutions. Therefore attention to the correct procedure is of the utmost importance if thorough fixation of albumen prints is to be achieved. An explanation of the mechanisms of fixation and of the removal of harmful by-products of fixation will be found in Chapters 9 and 11.

The basic approach to fixing albumen prints is to use two fixing baths, both of which must be freshly made up the day on which they will be used. The prints should be uniformly wetted by the fixer and agitated constantly during the fixation process. After 4 minutes in the first fixer they should be drained for at least 5 seconds and placed in a second tray of fresh fixer for an additional 4 minutes. The reason for the use of two-bath fixation is that some of the reaction products of silver chloride and sodium thiosulfate are insoluble in water and thus would never wash out of the print. The sulfur contained in these insoluble reaction products would eventually be released to attack and fade the silver image. However, these compounds—which are not soluble in water—are soluble in fresh sodium thiosulfate, and can be easily removed if there is a sufficient excess of fresh "hypo." This is the reason for the use of two fixing solutions.

It is important to make the fixing solutions slightly alkaline by adding 2 grams of sodium carbonate to each liter of fixing solution. This promotes more effective fixation and helps to prevent the blistering of the albumen layer on heavily albumenized papers. Another cause of blistering is too rapid changes in the temperature of processing solutions, so it is best to keep all solutions, including the fixer, at about 70°F (21° C). If blisters do appear, they do not spoil the prints in every case; if the blisters remain small they will sometimes disappear in drying, but if they are large or break, then the prints are usually ruined. Changes of temperature or pH of solutions are the main causes of blisters, but if they continually appear in spite of remedial measures, then there may be a problem of something in the rawstock reacting with the processing solutions. In that case a different rawstock will be needed.

When fixing is complete, the prints should be given a short wash (2 to 4 minutes) in running water and transferred to a hypo clearing agent solution at normal working strength. Either Kodak Hypo Clearing Agent™ or preferably, a 1% solution of sodium sulfite may be used for this purpose. After treatment in the hypo clearing agent the prints should receive a final wash for 30 minutes in an effective print washer. A large tray with a siphon arrangement will effectively wash one or two prints, but cannot satisfactorily handle more than that unless the prints are hand agitated during the entire washing period. To dry the prints a good approach is to gently blot them between acid-free blotters and allow them to air dry face up on fiberglass screens. Warm air may be used to accelerate drying.

CHAPTER 5

ALTERNATIVE AND
HYBRID PAPERS

The effect is the most artistic yet obtained on any paper of any make.

—Advertisement for "Albumat" brand
matte albumen paper, 1912[1]

———————

Three basic kinds of salted papers—plain salted, arrowroot and albumen—have already been described in this book. These materials are of landmark historical importance and also are fundamental to any modern practice with handmade silver printing out papers. However, they do not represent all of the possibilities of salted papers as a group. There are many alternative materials and techniques available which offer a very wide range of textures, colors, effects and contrasts. This chapter presents these alternative printing papers together with the historical context to which they belonged.

The handling and processing of these papers is generally the same as for the other salted papers already covered, but differences in processing will be noted. The main differences lie in the materials and techniques of coating the raw paper with organic binders to carry the silver image. Among the possible alternate materials useful as binders are whey[2], casein[3], agar-agar[4], carrageenin (Irish moss)[5], Iceland moss[6], and various resins[7]. Each of these materials has a characteristic effect on the printing process, and many different printing papers may also be created by *combining* these various binder substances. Even if only one kind of binder is used, a whole range of effects may be accomplished by simply varying the dilution, i.e. the amount, of binder that is applied to the raw paper.

The most important historical example of this is albumen paper, which has been used in many different dilutions over the course of photographic history. Pure albumen produces the familiar glossy albumen paper, while 1:1 dilutions (with water) result in a half-matte paper. A dilution of 1:6 produces a paper that is almost indistinguishable from other matte salted papers. Even a 2% solution of albumen causes a significant improvement in depth and contrast over a paper that is simply salted and has no organic binder at all. Many early photographic prints were made with diluted albumen as a conscious choice over pure albumen. Some photographers preferred the diluted albumen because it was easier to tone, though many chose matte papers for aesthetic reasons.

As outlined in Chapter 3, the earliest printing papers were salted with only a plain solution of salt water and depended on organic sizing such as starch or gelatin already present in the paper to favorably affect the printing process. When the value of organic binders was realized, the salting step became a "salting-sizing" step, whereby suitable organic substances were coated onto the paper to give increased density and detail. Among the very first organic materials to be tried for this purpose were gelatin (ca. 1850)[8], albumen (1850) and starch (1854). Less important, though also tried and used in the early 1850's was whey, or "serum of milk," of which the active sizing ingredient was lactose (milk sugar). During the period 1850-1855 fewer and fewer prints were made using only a plain salt solution; after 1855 most of the leading photographers were employing a salting-sizing solution based on the use of albumen in some dilution, gelatin, starch or whey. The majority of prints from the mid-1850's are matte, but not the very deep matte of simple salted paper. Also at this time the paper manufacturers were becoming aware of the photographic uses of their products, and some even offered specially sized and salted papers for photographic printing use.[9]

The first 25 years of photographic history were a period of very intense exploration of the possibilities of photographic materials, and printing papers were no exception. When the value of sizing on printing papers became clear, a wide variety of gums, sugars, starches, proteins, resins and other substances were tried. Of course most of these experiments yielded little or no improvement on established procedures, but the variety of *published* recipes alone is enormous, and sufficient to suggest that experimentation was the order of the day. Unlike later years when photographic techniques were conceived and maintained as proprietary secrets, the discoveries of this period were printed in journals and freely circulated, and this helped to further stimulate individual experimentation. Although indispensable to the evolution of photography as an art and science, all of this individual experimentation has created a very difficult situation for 20th-century curators and photographic conservators. These people are now charged with the formidable challenge of identification, and in some cases restoration, of these early prints.

The problem of process identification—not only for these early prints but for many much later prints—is very serious for the collector and curator as well as for the conservator. The attribution of a print to a specific photographer or the dating of a print may depend on a reliable process identification, but such an identification with salted papers is very difficult and in many cases impossible without resorting to destructive testing. Matte salted papers present this difficulty more often than glossy papers do, because with glossy papers there is usually enough binder material on the print to display that material's unique characteristics. For example, glossy albumen paper can usually be distinguished from gelatin printing-out paper fairly easily.

In the case of matte papers, materials are present in smaller quantities and tend to resemble each other, and differences in toning methods often obscure whatever clues the color of the image may provide. To make matters worse for the conservator, matte salted paper prints from this early period are very often the ones needing the most attention and care. At this point the knowledge and techniques to restore these prints are only beginning to be developed, and much more work and study need to be done. The first step is to understand from the historical context the complexity of the problem.

By 1865 the often confusing characteristics of printing-out papers had been fairly well established through experience and study, and some standardization of methods had been accomplished. Glossy albumen paper had become the most commonly used printing paper, and the bulk of it was no longer albumenized by the consumer, but in factories organized for the purpose. Factory-albumenized paper, though still prepared essentially by hand, was reasonably consistent in its appearance and results. It was welcomed as a time-saving alternative at first, and finally came to be regarded as a necessity. Most photographic manuals published after 1865 warn the novice photographer to avoid undue frustration and select his paper ready-made. However, many experienced photographers, especially those whose experience pre-dated the appearance of factory-made albumen and arrowroot papers, continued to produce their own salted papers.

During the last third of the 19th century the public at large and most professional photographers preferred glossy paper of various kinds (with albumen paper foremost until the early 90's), and matte salted papers became the province of those select professionals and amateurs who pursued photography as a means of artistic expression. Although most of the papers described in this chapter were pioneered in the 1850's and 1860's, they did not receive much attention until the late 1880's and 1890's, when salted papers enjoyed a revival, and a reaction set in against glossy papers among a whole new generation of photographers with a noncommercial, nonscientific orientation. As beautiful as glossy albumen paper could be, it became identified with the mediocre productions of commercial portrait studios, among which producing the glossiest possible prints seemed to be a matter of professional pride. The hand-coated matte salted papers were now seen as an attractive alternative, especially after new methods of platinum toning opened a whole range of brown and black image colors that were never possible before (see Chapter 8).

The salted paper revival began with photographers coating their own paper, but in the 1880's a number of matte salted papers appeared on the market and became modestly popular. Plain salted and arrowroot papers had never completely disappeared from trade lists, but among new types of paper were the so-called "Algeinpapiere" (made from Iceland moss), several different resin papers (made with mixed resin-gelatin and resin-starch binders) and matte albumen papers (made with mixtures of albumen and starch). These various matte salted papers were mainly produced in Europe by already established producers of albumen paper, and it appears that few, if any, were exported to the United States. Most of these papers were available in either sensitized or unsensitized condition.

One element which contributed to the salted paper revival was the popularity during the 1880's of true platinum prints, which many photographers admired but few could afford as the price of platinum soared in the early 1890's. It turned out to be cheaper to tone a silver print with a platinum toner than to make an actual platinotype print. Several manufacturers saw a marketing opportunity in this and offered matte salted papers under names like "silver-platinum paper,"[10] etc. The finished prints somewhat resembled true platinotypes, but always retained certain characteristics of silver salted papers.

Matte albumen papers were the most popular commercial article of all the papers described in this chapter,[11] but at their peak in the years preceding World War I they accounted for only a small percentage of the total photographic paper market. They faced competition from the many other "artistic" printing methods available at the time—platinum, gum bichromate, carbon printing, matte collodion emulsion-type papers,—and all matte salted papers also bore the stigma of alleged impermanence. Whether justified or not, the reputation of silver papers as impermanent was not helped by the advertising campaigns mounted by the manufacturers of carbon and platinum materials. By the end of the 1920's all matte salted papers were out of commercial production and belonged to the history of photography.[12]

Resin Papers

Resins were used as paper sizing (including photographic rawstocks) for most of the 19th century. The use of resins as an internal sizing for paper suggested that they could be adapted as an after-sizing for salted papers, and the idea was tried as early as the 1860's. One of the drawbacks to this idea was that thick deposits of resins are impermeable and the print can be toned, fixed and washed only with great difficulty. Also the yellow color of some resins together with a tendency of some batches of rosin to discolor after sensitization kept resin papers from wide use. In the 1880's resin papers were improved when Henry Cooper of England suggested a mixture of resin and gelatin be used instead of pure resins.[13] This yielded a matte paper that gave soft results similar to platinum prints, especially when a black color was obtained through the use of combined gold and platinum toning.

The basis of resin papers is that a resin soap (made with a resin and an alkali) is combined with a soluble chloride and mixed with either gelatin or starch. This mixture is coated on paper and allowed to dry. When the paper is sensitized on a silver nitrate solution, the resin is precipitated and becomes insoluble, analogous to the way albumen is rendered insoluble on contact with silver nitrate. One of the most simple resin papers is this one, made with shellac and arrowroot:

RESIN-ARROWROOT PAPER
This preparation (according to the method described in 1896 by A. von Hübl),[14] can be used with most kinds of rawstocks; for well-sized,

smooth rawstocks use the recommended amount of shellac solution, and for porous rawstocks up to double the recommended amount may be used. The first step is to prepare a shellac-ammonia solution by the following method: In a porcelain or enamel pan pour 100 ml water over 10 g powdered white shellac, then add 5 ml strong ammonia **(CAUTION! Wear eye protection and work in a well ventilated area!)** and heat with stirring until the solution is uniform. This solution will keep. Next make 100 ml of 2.5% arrowroot solution that contains 2.5 g sodium chloride. Make this according to the method of preparing an arrowroot solution given in Chapter 3. With vigorous stirring or shaking add 10 ml of the ammonia-shellac solution to the arrowroot solution. Pin the paper to a flat board and distribute the salting mixture evenly with a wide flat brush or a foam brush. With a dry brush smooth out and evenly distribute the coating until a uniform matte appearance is obtained, and hang the paper to dry in a warm place.

Sensitize the paper by floating it for 4 or 5 minutes on a silver solution made as follows:

SILVER NITRATE	120 g
CITRIC ACID	80 g
DISTILLED WATER	1 liter

Although it is quite possible to tone the prints with gold toning baths, Hübl recommends toning them in a platinum toner (see Chapter 8). Combined gold and platinum toning (with gold first) will produce a neutral black tone, while platinum toner used alone will produce a succession of tones from reddish brown to black with reddish-violet cast. Prolonged platinum toning will lead to yellowing of the highlights. Other processing steps are done according to the general outline of processing for salted papers given at the end of Chapter 3.

Matte Albumen Paper

Matte albumen paper refers to a matte salted paper that has been prepared with a mixture of albumen and starch. It was the invention of Baron Arthur von Hübl, an Austrian who did a great deal to further the use of matte salted papers. Hübl also wrote extensively on the platinum printing process and on technical photographic matters Hübl's book on matte salted papers, *Der Silberdruck auf Salzpapier* (Silver Printing on Salted Paper) was published in 1896. Although unfortunately it was never translated into English the book remains the most complete and well written book on matte salted papers ever to appear. Many of the formulae he freely published in *Der Silberdruck auf Salzpapier* later made a great deal of money for photographic paper manufacturers.

Figure 27.
Advertisement for matte albumen paper in **Paris Photo Gazette**, *April 25, 1909.*

The original formula for matte-albumen paper was first published by Hübl in the journal *Photographische Rundschau* for Feb. 1895, and it described a paper made with a mixture of equal volumes of albumen and a 2% arrowroot solution. In 1898 the firm of E. Just in Vienna brought on the market a ready-sensitized paper based on Hübl's formula.[15] In 1902 the long-established albumen paper manufacturer Trapp and Munch followed suit. The new product caught on with portrait photographers and partially revived a badly sagging market for the albumen paper producers. Many other companies started making matte albumen paper, giving their products names like Alboidin, Albumon, and Albumat.[16] For the first few years the paper was made according to the original formula—which produced a deep matte surface—but in 1913 a half-matte paper appeared[17]; this was apparently accomplished by increasing the proportion of albumen in the salting solution. Following the taste of the day, most manufacturers of matte albumen paper offered an extremely wide choice of base stocks. Trapp and Munch offered 18 different choices, including Chinese and Japanese paper, several weights and colors, and a number of different textures.

Matte albumen paper found its chief commercial application among the more sophisticated (and expensive) portrait photographers of the time. Because the toning influenced the color of the print so completely—it was brownish red in the absence of any toning, purplish-black with only gold toning and warm brown to black with combined gold and platinum toning—there was ample opportunity to suit the color of the image to the overall feel of the portrait. Writers in photographic trade magazines rhapsodized over the similarities between matte albumen paper and the more "elegant" and "artistic" processes such as gum bichromate and platinum printing. Matte albumen paper was regarded as a great convenience compared to those processes which it allegedly resembled, but of course by modern business standards in the photographic portrait industry it would be seen as only slightly easier than printing an original portrait in oils.

Although matte albumen paper was mainly produced and consumed in Germany, it was exported to the rest of Europe in the years before World War 1[18]; whether it reached American shores in any quantity during those years is unclear. Matte gelatin printing-out papers (produced by adding resins, starches or clays to the normal emulsion formulae) were much used in the United States and were toned by the same techniques used for matte albumen paper, hence confusion between the two materials is possible. In most cases, however, matte albumen paper will be found to have a slightly rougher, more matte surface than matte gelatin paper. After World War I the market for matte albumen paper declined sharply, because the austere economic conditions in Germany did not favor a printing paper that required precious metal toning. The last company to produce matte albumen paper was Trapp & Münch. They ceased production of it in 1929, issuing a brief statement saying that their "gaslight" developing-out paper (with the somewhat bizarre name of "Tuma-Gas") was in every way a worthy substitute.[19] This announcement apparently marks the last time albumen paper of any sort was offered to the public; the last date of manufacture of the older glossy albumen paper was probably ca. 1926.

PREPARATION OF MATTE ALBUMEN PAPER

The following method of preparing matte albumen paper was described by Hübl in his book, *Der Silderdruck auf Salzpapier.*[20] Matte albumen paper is prepared from fresh albumen; the freshest possible eggs are carefully separated, and the whites beaten to a froth just as in the preparation of the usual glossy variety of albumen paper described in Chapter 4. However, the albumen is not allowed to age—rather it is used at most 24 hours after it has settled back to a liquid state. It should be kept refrigerated during settling and filtered through muslin immediately before use. To prepare the salting solution combine 100 ml of fresh albumen with 100 ml of arrowroot solution prepared according to the instructions given in Chapter 3. The 100 ml of arrowroot solution should contain 4 g of sodium chloride.

Very porous rawstocks such as watercolor paper, etc., may require a pre-sizing with plain arrowroot to obtain the best results, but for most papers pre-sizing is not necessary. Pin the sheet of paper to be coated to a flat surface and distribute the arrowroot-albumen mixture according to the procedures outlined for arrowroot papers in Chapter 3. Hang the coated sheets to dry in a warm room. The coated paper will keep indefinitely if stored flat in a cool and dry place. To sensitize the paper float it for 1 to 2 minutes on a solution composed of:

SILVER NITRATE	120 g
CITRIC ACID	15 g
DISTILLED WATER	TO MAKE 1 liter

Paper thus sensitized will keep in good condition for several weeks, depending on the temperature and humidity of the storage environment. An alternative method of sensitization is to brush the silver solution on the paper with a wide, flat brush. Two brushings—allowing the paper to dry in between brushings—may be necessary to obtain sufficient strength of image. Shadow areas will be weak when sensitization has been insufficient.

It is very important to success with matte albumen paper to ensure that the paper is not too dry at the time of printing. Excessive dryness of the paper will result in flat and weak prints. Conditioning the paper in a damp environment such as a basement or closed box with a dish of water inside will probably be necessary in order to obtain the best results. A special kind of blotting paper called "Hygro-Papier" was manufactured and sold by Trapp & Münch for use with matte albumen paper.[21] The "Hygro-Papier" was dampened and placed behind the matte albumen paper in the printing frame to insure that a high level of moisture was maintained. Proper pre-conditioning of the sensitized paper should make such measures as "Hygro-Papier" unnecessary, however.

Matte albumen paper requires a negative of about the same density range as glossy albumen paper. The processing of matte albumen paper is the same as with most other kinds of salted paper, and the general outline given at the end of Chapter 3 should be followed. Care should be taken to insure a thorough initial wash that removes as much of the silver nitrate as possible. Most of the gold or platinum toners given in Chapter 8 will work on matte albumen paper. If combined gold and platinum toning is used, deep brown of brown-violet tones may be obtained. Matte albumen paper generally tones faster than glossy albumen paper. Fixing, washing and drying are the same as with most other salted papers.

CHAPTER 6

SENSITIZATION

The change of sensitised paper in the dark is found a serious evil by practical photographers. I know some persons, who, from this cause, waste as much paper as they use.

—C.A. SEELY, 1860[1]

• ———————————— •

The sensitization step, in which the previously "salted" papers are rendered light sensitive by treatment with a silver nitrate solution, is vitally important to successful printing with albumen and salted papers. This chapter is devoted to the solutions and procedures employed for this purpose. The composition of the sensitizing solution may include other substances such as citric acid, but it always has one basic ingredient: silver nitrate. Silver nitrate is formed by the action of nitric acid on silver metal. It is sold in the form of colorless crystals, normally in quantities of 1 ounce, 4 ounces, and 1 pound. As with nearly all chemicals, a considerable saving is realized by buying in large amounts, and the one-pound package is economical compared to the one-ounce size. For albumen and salted paper printing a "technical" or "ACS" grade is sufficiently pure, and there is no need to purchase the highly purified grades that are required in photographic emulsion making.

The primary light-sensitive substance in all the papers described in this book is silver chloride. Silver chloride is always formed *in situ* by a "double replacement" reaction between whatever chloride is used to "salt" the paper—sodium chloride, for example—and silver nitrate. In a "double replacement" reaction the ions of two compounds change partners, forming two new substances. The reaction between sodium chloride and silver nitrate yields sodium nitrate and silver chloride. Since silver chloride is nearly insoluble in water it is immediately precipitated as a cloudy white mass. A chemist might symbolically write the reaction this way:

$$NaCl + AgNO_3 \longrightarrow NaNO_3 + AgCl \downarrow$$

Sodium chloride and Silver nitrate produce sodium nitrate and silver chloride.

The symbol $\downarrow$ means that the silver chloride is precipitated; the sodium nitrate which is formed is a soluble substance and remains in solution. Sodium nitrate has no effect on the printing process and is washed away during processing.

For reasons explained in Chapter 1 there must be sufficient silver nitrate in the sensitizing solution not only to react with all the chloride present on the paper, but also to leave a considerable excess of silver nitrate present in the light-sensitive layer. In practice the silver nitrate solution must be approximately four times as strong as the original salting solution. If a 3% salting solution was used, then the strength of the sensitizing solution must be approximately 12%, depending in part on the type of binder material used on the paper (see below). The sensitizing solution itself must be made with distilled or at least de-ionized water, because if made with tap water, the silver nitrate will react with chlorine and "hard water ions" such as carbonates, etc., that exist in many water supplies. The result is a cloudy white precipitate of silver chloride, silver carbonate, etc., which robs the bath of strength and makes sensitizing difficult. During the initial wash step of processing albumen and salted papers, the clouding of the water which occurs is this very reaction between the excess silver nitrate left in the paper and various ions present in tap water.

———

Composition of the Sensitizing Solution

CAUTION:
Always wear eye protection when compounding or handling silver nitrate solutions!

The simplest sensitizing solution may be made as follows:

SILVER NITRATE	120 g
DISTILLED WATER	TO MAKE 1 liter

The strength of the silver solution for any given paper is governed by several factors; the first is the amount of chloride that has been used to "salt" the paper. In general less "salting" requires a less strong silver bath and vice versa. For most salted papers it is best to keep the chloride content at about 2-2.5% and the silver bath at 10-12%, because lowering the chloride content tends to produce prints that lack brilliance and density. Albumen paper is a somewhat different case, in that the presence of the glossy albumen surface tends to compensate for a lack of a heavy deposit of image silver. By lowering the chloride content of albumen paper to the range of 1-1.5% thinner negatives may be more successfully printed, and a weaker silver bath—in the area of 8-9%—is called for. Such a low chloride content and weak silver bath were commonly used in the period 1880-1900 to try to accommodate the negatives with relatively lower density ranges produced by gelatin dry plates. On the whole, however, modern practice with albumen paper is best conducted with a chloride content of 1.5% or above and a silver bath strength of 10% or above. Of course, this means that some thin negatives will not be printable. This is a small loss, because better looking and more permanent prints will result from the increased silver image deposited by stronger salting and silvering (see Chapter 11).

A second consideration in the strength of the silver solution is the nature of the binder material used. For papers in which starch is the binder material strong silver baths and short times of floating on the sensitizing solution are required. The reason for this is that unlike albumen, starch is not coagulated or rendered insoluble by the silver solution. Too long floatation will cause a loss in image brilliance because the starch layer is very permeable to water and absorption of fine silver chloride particles down into the paper fibers is more likely if floatation is prolonged. Also, the strength of the sensitizing solution regulates the size of the grains of precipitated silver chloride; stronger solutions produce larger grains that are less likely to be absorbed into the paper fibers. Hence for arrowroot and matte albumen papers strong silver baths and short floatation times are required.[2]

The duration of the floating of albumen paper on the sensitizing solution depends partly on the strength of that solution. If the silver bath is very strong, the coagulating effect of silver nitrate on the albumen layer is correspondingly strong, and the solution will not permeate through the albumen very quickly. This means that a longer time of floatation is required for albumen paper on strong sensitizing solutions. On the other hand if the silver solution is relatively weak, then prolonged floating may be detrimental because the albumen—which is water soluble unless coagulated—may begin to dissolve off the sheet before it is completely coagulated. This phenomenon is especially noticeable with freshly made-up sensitizing baths, because the sodium or ammonium nitrate which accumulates in older baths as a result of the "double replacement" reaction involved is absent when a bath is fresh. These salts also have a coagulating effect on albumen, and some old manuals advise actually adding some ammonium or sodium nitrate to sensitizing baths to insure proper coagulation of the albumen. However, this advice pertained to relatively silver-poor baths of 5 to 8%, and is not applicable when a bath of 10% strength is used.

Techniques of Sensitization

CAUTION:
Always wear approved eye protection and tightly fitting surgeon's gloves during the operations of sensitizing paper.

Silver nitrate can cause permanent, irreversible eye damage. Although infrequent contact with silver nitrate and the resulting staining of the skin does not appear to be dangerous to health, prolonged exposure can lead to permanent staining of the skin. Ultimately silver absorbed through the skin will be deposited in various locations around the body causing irreversible staining of the conjunctivae, blood vessel walls, gums, mucous membranes, etc. This condition is known as *argyria*. Consequences more serious than staining of the tissues have also been reported, and all necessary precautions should be taken to avoid repeated absorption of silver nitrate through the skin. Always wash hands immediately after contact with the silver nitrate solution. The most important precaution, however, is to wear eye protection; sheets dripping silver solution pose a special hazard to eyes.

THE FLOATATION METHOD OF SENSITIZATION
The operation of sensitizing and drying must always be conducted under proper safelight illumination. See Chapter 2 for details on appropriate workroom lighting. An average time of floatation of albumen paper on the sensitizing solution is 2½ to 3 minutes. This

ensures adequate sensitization of even doubly albumenized paper. Albumen paper should not be excessively dry at the time of sensitization. Conditioning the paper by storing it overnight in a damp basement or placing it for a few hours in a closed box with a dish of water will confer two benefits in the sensitizing procedure: first, it will allow the albumen layer to evenly take up the sensitizing solution and second, the sheets will not be so stiff and hard to manipulate. The most common approach to applying the sensitizing solution to the sheet is floating. The actual technique of floating is no different from the floatation methods described in Chapter 3 for applying the sizing-salting solutions. Care in necessary to prevent the silver solution from reaching the back of the sheets, since patches of uneven density may result. A three-minute egg timer is a handy accessory when sensitizing paper. Always time the duration of floating from the moment all bubbles have been broken and the sheet lies flat on the surface of the solution. The bubbles that appear usually originate from air trapped under the sheet or are formed by the droplets draining from a previous sheet. Blowing gently on the bubbles before floating the sheet usually bursts them, or at least moves them to the side of the tray.

Figure 28.
Table for sensitizing paper. A is a sheet of paper hung to dry after sensitizing, together with a small dish underneath to catch the drippings. B is the tray containing the sensitizer. C is a sheet waiting to be sensitized, and D is a cushion holding pins used to hang the sensitized sheets.

Ideally, the tray, and all containers used for the silver solution, should be made of glass. A stainless steel tray is not recommended. If a plastic tray has to be used, it should be new, because plastic tends to hold on to chemicals; unwanted staining could be the result of a tray contaminated with developer or fixer from ordinary photographic work. Pyrex™ baking dishes are not precisely the right size for the usual negative formats, but are serviceable. A glass rod is also a handy accessory when sensitizing paper. It is useful for bursting stubborn bubbles and for lifting the corners of the sheets when it is time to remove them from the silver solution. The lifting of the sheets should be performed very slowly in order to allow the silver solution to drain evenly off the sheet. Lift one corner of the sheet and gently and slowly peel it off the surface. When the sheet has been properly lifted, hardly a drop will leave the sheet while it is held in the air over the tray to drain. The sheets should be hung from clothespins by two corners of the long edge so that the runoff has the shortest distance to travel. Inclining the line at an angle of 5-7 degrees allows the runoff to collect at one corner where it can be conveniently blotted. Blotting of the drops that form on the lower corner is essential to speedy drying and even sensitization. Do not over dry the sensitized paper; albumen paper will become brittle if excessively dry, and most salted papers—especially matte albumen paper—will not produce satisfactory prints if they are too dry.

BRUSH SENSITIZATION

With matte salted papers—but not glossy albumen paper—an alternative method of sensitization is to brush on the sensitizing solution. This has the advantages of requiring less made-up silver nitrate solution and of doing away with the danger of getting sensitizer on the back of the sheet. However, brush sensitizing has the disadvantage of the constant possibility of streaks resulting from uneven application of the sensitizer. Brush coating should be performed with a wide, flat Japanese brush, one in which the bristles are bound with thread rather than a metal ferrule. The reason for this is that the silver nitrate will react with the metal of the ferrule and cause stains in the print.

Slightly stronger solutions are employed in brush coating than in sensitization by floating. The brush should be well washed with distilled water after each use and reserved exclusively for sensitization. The brush will soon be discolored but this will not affect its performance, if it is kept clean. Another way to apply the sensitizing solution is with a "Blanchard's brush," which consists of a 4-inch wide, ¼-inch thick piece of wood or Plexiglas™, over which are stretched several folds of clean flannel. Sanding smooth corners on the working edge of the wood or Plexiglas™ strip is helpful. Dip the

Blanchard's brush into the silver solution and apply it to the paper with smooth even strokes.

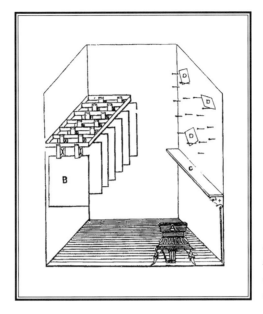

Figure 29.

Figure 29.
A drying room for
sensitized paper. A small
stove can be seen at right

Two applications may be needed if sufficient density cannot be obtained in shadow areas of the print, especially with papers coated with a relatively heavy layer of binder material. The appearance of blotches or light spots in dense areas of the print is a phenomenon described in old manuals as the "measles," and is caused by insufficient sensitization. This trouble may appear in either floated or brush-coated papers. The cause may either be a too-weak silver solution or insufficient residual sensitizing solution in the paper. Nothing can be done for prints that already have been exposed, but unexposed sheets suspected of having the same difficulty may be re-floated or rebrushed with a stronger sensitizing solution. The appearance of paper-white round spots with hard, definite edges is the result of air bubbles trapped under the sheet during floating on the sensitizing solution; these areas have therefore not been sensitized at all. Similar white spots also arise when air bubbles prevent the sizing-salting solution from covering an area of the print, but instead of being paper-white they typically have a light brown stain from the action of the silver nitrate.

EXHAUSTION OF THE SILVER SOLUTION

After some sheets have been sensitized by the floating method—which in most cases is the best and most satisfactory approach—the remaining silver solution will be reduced in both strength and volume. The strength of the silver solution will be lowered by the reaction of the silver nitrate with the chlorides in the paper, and the volume will be reduced by the simple mechanical absorption of silver solution by the sheets of paper as they are floated. Although the amount of silver nitrate removed from the bath by both causes remains fairly constant and predictable, in practice a relatively weak bath needs more constant attention and replenishment than a relatively strong one does, since the weaker bath is brought to a dysfunctional point more rapidly. It is bothersome to be constantly monitoring and replenishing a silver solution, so it is better to start with a 12% bath and attempt to maintain it in a range of 10-12%, where there need be little concern over insufficient sensitization or the "measles." Of course, 10% baths are less expensive than 12% ones, but the lost time and expense of inadvertently spoiled sheets and frequent determinations of the strength of the solution make the relatively weaker baths a false economy. The 12% solution will remain functional and satisfactory for perhaps two or three batches of prints—say a total of 30 11 x 14 prints—before a determination of strength need be made, whereas the 10% bath will need replenishing much sooner.

Obviously, it is necessary somehow to determine the strength of the solution and replace its lost strength and volume long before such drastic consequences as insensitive, flat prints or the "measles" make their appearance. The most accurate approach is to periodically chemically analyze the silver content of the solution by means of a titration analysis (see below), but this is not always possible. In the absence of a reliable means of testing the silver content, a rule of thumb for replenishment may be used instead, and fairly reliable results obtained. This rule of thumb may be summarized as follows: Replenish the lost volume with a silver nitrate solution twice as strong as the original bath. For example, if the original strength and volume were 1 liter of 12% silver solution and after a printing session only 850 ml remained, replenish with 150 ml of 24% silver solution. This should restore the silver bath to the original strength and volume. If citric acid is used in the sensitizing solution, it is replenished strictly on the basis of volume lost from the solution. For example, if the liter of sensitizing solution had originally contained 5% citric acid (i.e., 50 g) and 850 ml was left after a printing session, then the missing 15% of the original volume of 1 liter represents a loss of 15%

(i.e., 7.5 g) of citric acid. Thus the 150 ml of replenisher would contain 7.5 g citric acid in addition to the required amount of silver nitrate.

The rule of thumb method of replenishment is not suitable for continuous use, or when a large amount of printing is to be done. The errors which are inherent in the method may accumulate with unpleasant and expensive results. For more critical and serious work the best method is to analyze the silver content of the bath using a titration procedure. The following adaptation of a classical procedure in quantitative analysis requires a modest outlay for equipment but affords accurate, speedy determinations. After the initial calibrations have been performed, a determination of silver-bath strength can be made in only a few minutes. In practice, a determination is required only about every third printing session, unless a great many sheets are sensitized at one time. The details of these procedures were worked out by Irving Pobboravsky, a research technologist at the Graphic Arts Research Center at Rochester Institute of Technology, and have been successfully used by the author for several years. They appear here through the permission of Mr. Pobboravsky.

The method consists in slowly adding a reagent solution (sodium thiocyanate) to a measured amount of silver solution mixed with an "indicator" (ferric ammonium sulfate) until a color change takes place that cannot be made to disappear by stirring or agitation. To make sure that only the desired reactions take place between the silver nitrate, the sodium thiocyanate and the "indicator," the silver solution is acidified with a small quantity of nitric acid. At the point of the irreversible color change, the amount of the thiocyanate consumed indirectly tells the concentration of the silver nitrate solution. The method is known as Volhard's method (after the 19th-century chemist who discovered it), and it was in use for the purpose of keeping track of albumen paper sensitizing baths as early as 1875. The complete working details of the method may be found in Appendix B.

DECOLORIZING THE SILVER SOLUTION

It will become apparent after the first printing session with albumen or salted papers that although the silver solution begins as a perfectly clear and colorless solution, it soon turns brown and eventually almost black with use. The cause of this is the fact that some organic matter from the sizing of the paper or whatever organic binder is used—albumen, gelatin, etc.—always partially dissolves into the silver solution. The reaction of this organic matter with some of the silver of the sensitizing solution eventually causes a spontaneous reduction of the reacted silver to the metallic state. The metallic silver is responsible for the coloration of the solution. In much the same way a sensitized but unexposed sheet of albumen paper will spontaneously "print-out" over time and become dark brown.

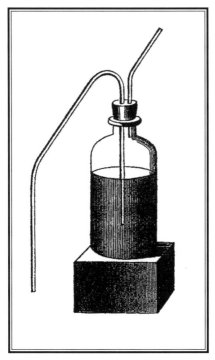

Figure 30.

Siphon apparatus for use in decolorizing silver solutions. A siphon was used to extract the decolorized silver solution without disturbing the layer of powdered kaolin on the bottom.

The silver solution may be used in a slightly discolored state, but not when it is nearly black. Some way must be found to remove this organic material or the silver bath quickly becomes useless. The best way is to use a finely powdered white clay known as kaolin, which if shaken up with the bath, will absorb the organic matter and settle to the bottom of the bottle, thus clearing the solution. About 15 grams of kaolin is sufficient to repeatedly clear one liter of silver solution. The kaolin should be left in the container in which the silver bath is stored, and after each use, the bath and kaolin should be shaken up together. The kaolin will settle out overnight and the bath will be clear and ready to use the next day.

To avoid the difficulty of trying to decant the clarified solution, a siphon arrangement like the one pictured can be easily constructed.

All that is required is a two-hole rubber stopper and some glass tubing. To cut glass tubing, first score it with a file and snap at the score line, then round the sharp edges on a gas flame. To use the siphon, blow in the short tube to start the flow, and the bottle will empty itself down to the level of the bottom of the drain tube without disturbing the kaolin in the bottom of the bottle. If for some reason there is not time to allow the kaolin to settle out of the silver bath, the kaolin may be removed by filtering the solution through medium filter paper. If a silver bath has acquired a surface scum which shows up either in the tray or as a metallic marbled sheen on exposed prints, filtering the solution is necessary. *Always* make sure that the surface of the silver solution is free from scum before floating a sheet of paper.

———•———

Preserving Sensitized Paper

Under normal circumstances albumen and salted papers will remain usable only for one or two days after sensitization. In extremely humid and warm conditions they may yellow in a matter of 8 to 12 hours, or even less. The yellow color is actually spontaneously reduced metallic silver in a very finely divided state. As the process of spontaneous reduction of silver continues, the paper turns a deep reddish brown; ultimately the paper turns black with a shiny greenish "bronzed" surface. It may require several months to reach the "bronzed" stage in dark storage. The spontaneous reduction of silver can be slowed by storing the sensitized paper in a tightly closed container in a cool and dry place, since air and moisture accelerate the process of decomposition. Papers that are only slightly yellowed may still be usable, because the fixer will remove some of the finely divided silver from the highlight areas.

Naturally the rapid decomposition of sensitized papers is a real inconvenience in printing operations. For best results it is necessary to sensitize, print and process all on the same day. There does exist an alternative procedure, in which organic acids are either added to the silver nitrate solution or applied to the paper in a separate step (this can be done before or after sensitization). The most effective organic acid for this purpose is citric acid, which is also used in many foodstuffs as a preservative. Citric acid has a marked effect on those papers such as arrowroot or resin-arrowroot, which do not contain an "active" organic binder substance. In these papers it produces a redder, more brilliant print than would otherwise be obtained, and it incidentally preserves them a little longer after sensitization.

The addition of 5% citric acid to the silver bath produces the maximum preservative effect, although as little as 1% will extend usable life to a noticeable extent. In the case of glossy albumen paper the addition of citric acid to either the albumen or the sensitizing solution has an effect on the color of the print, causing it to become reddish brown, even with prolonged gold toning. When the citric acid is present in the silver nitrate solution, the print color seems to be more brownish than when the citric acid is present in the albumen. In both cases, however, the pre-processing stability of albumen paper is improved, and greater sensitivity and maximum density are achieved. The preservative effects of citric acid were known as early as 1860[3], but apparently it was not realized that by increasing the amount of citric acid in the silver solution, greatly improved stability could be obtained.

The idea of using a large amount of citric acid in the sensitizing solution to preserve albumen paper was first published in 1869 by a Viennese photographer named Adolf Ost.[4] In 1872 the first "ready sensitized" albumen paper, a product of the Sensitized Paper Co. of Portsmouth, Ohio, was offered to the public.[5] Hailed as a great breakthrough, this invention promised to revolutionize the practice of albumen printing, and at least as far as amateur photographers were concerned, it did. Professionals, however, continued to sensitize their own paper for two reasons: purple tones were difficult to produce in the presence of the citric acid, and it was considerably cheaper to sensitize the paper "at home." Although the use of organic acids—citric, tartaric and oxalic—was the basis of most "ready sensi-

Figure 31.
An 1887 advertisement
for an albumen paper
sensitizing service.

✢ SENSITIZED ✢
ALBUMENIZED PAPER.
••••••••••••••••••••••••••••••••
Prints quickly. Tones easily. Results perfect.
••••••••••••••••••••••••••••••••
➼❋ MISS ✚ AMY ✚ SCOTT, ❋⬷
PRACTICAL SENSITIZER,
32 Upham Park Road, Chiswick, London.

THE ALBUMEN & SALTED PAPER BOOK

tized" papers, there were a number of ways in which the preservative effects could be obtained (see figure 31). The exact methods used by manufacturers of "ready sensitized" paper were jealously guarded secrets. With the advent of the gelatin dry plate in the 1880's there was a great upsurge of amateur photography and "ready sensitized" albumen paper gained enormously in popularity. Very few amateurs in the 1880's and 1890's bothered to sensitize their own paper.

TECHNIQUES FOR PRESERVING SENSITIZED
ALBUMEN AND SALTED PAPERS

As mentioned above, a serviceable technique that requires the least effort is simply to add 5% citric acid to the sensitizing bath. The formulae of many salted papers already stipulate this addition, and where it is not called for it may be used as an option for increased keeping qualities after sensitization. Alternative approaches are to brush a 2% citric acid solution on the paper either before applying the salting-sizing solution, or after sensitization. Papers to be "preserved" must be scrupulously kept out of white light, because the slightest exposure to actinic light forms some metallic silver that acts as a catalyst for further silver reduction.

Another technique for preserving paper in the 19th century was to wash out a considerable part of the residual silver nitrate after sensitization, then restore sensitivity immediately before printing by fuming with ammonia. For a modern worker to duplicate the 3- or 4-month useful life for albumen paper that commercial "ready sensitized" paper achieved in the 19th century would mean a long process of experimentation with silver bath strength, citric acid content, etc. The end result in the 19th century (as evidenced by many complaints in the journals) was often paper that was so silver-poor that it required a revitalizing treatment with ammonia fumes before even a barely satisfactory print could be obtained. As a general rule, albumen and salted papers deliver the best results when used as soon after sensitization as possible.

Ammonia and Other Additives
to the Silver Bath

In 1840 it was first noticed that adding ammonia to a silver bath until the brown precipitate which forms is finally re-dissolved causes a more brilliant, vigorous image in salted papers.[6] "Ammonia-nitrate" was particularly useful for printing from weak negatives. The "ammonia-nitrate" process was very widely used for salted papers in the period 1840-1860, but it had some disadvantages. The prints sensitized on an ammoniacal silver solution yellowed very quickly, and the solution itself tended to discolor very rapidly. Brush sensitizing lessened the latter difficulty, but the first one remained.

When albumen paper began to be used in the early 1850's, the disadvantages of the ammonia nitrate bath multiplied, since it tended to dissolve the albumen off the paper. Photographers tried to correct this by neutralizing the ammoniated bath with nitric acid, and this approach solved the problem. But in neutralizing the ammonia the real effect was to form ammonium nitrate, which builds up in use anyway, so the utility of adding ammonia then acidifying with nitric acid is doubtful, though it does appear to make a slight contribution to the sensitivity of the paper. Fuming seems to be a better way to produce the advantages of ammoniacal silver.

Many old manuals do recommend the use of ammonia—and a number of other substances—in the silver bath. Most of these are superfluous, if not potentially harmful. One clear danger in the use of ammonia in silver baths is the potential for the formation of fulminating silver, a highly explosive substance, if an ammoniacal silver bath is "boiled down," as some old manuals recommend.[7] "Boiling down" is supposed to be a way to rejuvenate a bath that has become overloaded with sodium or ammonium nitrates and organic matter, but the author has had no occasion to employ this procedure, and it is not recommended for anyone to undertake this dangerous operation.

The additives recommended by various 19th-century sources had three purposes: increased sensitivity, coagulation of the albumen layer, and preservation of the sensitized paper. For increasing sensitivity ammonia was the main substance recommended, but citric acid also has an effect on sensitivity, and this recommendation will be found in some manuals. The second class of additives—albumen coagulants—includes the largest and most wide-ranging list of substances. At various times sugar, camphor, alum, sodium, and ammonium nitrate and alcohol were all suggested. The third group of additives, intended to help preserve sensitized paper, has been dealt with above. For modern practice, only preservative additions are recommended.

Reclamation of Silver Wastes

Only about 6-8% of the silver initially present in a sheet of sensitized paper is utilized to form the image; the rest is washed or fixed away in processing. Much of the silver can be recovered by careful saving and treatment of the processing solutions. Most of the recoverable silver is found in the first and second changes of wash water. Where the volume of printing operations warrant, these should be saved and the silver precipitated out of them by adding either sodium chloride or sodium carbonate. The silver will then be in the form of insoluble silver chloride or silver carbonate, and after settling the excess water can be decanted off. A great deal of silver is present in the fixing solutions, and these should be placed in a large container and allowed to evaporate to a thick sludge, or to dryness when ready to ship to a refiner for processing. Print trimmings and spoiled prints are also a source of recoverable silver. They can be burned and silver (and gold) recovered from their ashes. All of these economy measures were in common use in the 19th century, especially by larger volume operations. In a typical gallery about 60% of the silver consumed was recovered, though in exceptional cases 75% or above was achieved.

All of the residues of wash water, fixer and print trimmings must be sent to a precious metal refiner for conversion back to pure silver. Sometimes volume users in the 19th century did their own smelting and refining, but most often the residues were sent out to be processed. Many of the larger photographic supply houses offered this service, in addition to converting the recovered silver back into silver nitrate. For modern printers who use only a small amount of silver and gold, silver recovery measures may not be economically feasible because of the high costs of refining. Many refiners have a minimum charge or specify minimum amounts of residues. Shipping charges must be borne by the consumer, adding to the cost of silver recovery. Smelting and re-nitrating silver are *not* operations for the home laboratory. Thus, unless a large amount of printing is done, silver recovery is usually not worth the trouble.

CHAPTER 7

TONE REPRODUCTION AND PRINT EXPOSURE

Now if we had complete control over the finished negative as to be able always to predetermine its character, we should unhesitatingly produce all negatives so that they would stand printing in sunshine for all or the principal part of the exposure to light. Somehow it appears that those prints are most admired which have had actual sunshine direct on the negative during all, or nearly all, the process.

—Thomas Bolas, 1889[1]

———— • ————

Those who have had experience in ordinary photographic processes know how important the developing step is in determining the density, contrast and even the color of the photographic image. In all printing-out papers—including albumen and salted papers—the "development" step is equally important in determining the color, density and contrast of the image; only instead of

Figure 32.
Printing frames in use.

varying with the composition of the developer or the time, temperature, etc., the image is affected by the color and intensity of the exposing light and the duration of exposure. In printing-out papers, exposure and development are simultaneous and inseparable. The exposure step is in many ways the most exciting aspect of printing with albumen and salted papers. It is quite a thrill to place a sheet of hand-coated paper in the printing frame for the first time and watch it darken, and it is a refreshing change to bring photographic processes out of the darkroom and into the sunshine. This chapter examines the relationship between negative characteristics and tone reproduction in albumen and salted papers as well as the theory and practice of print exposure.

Characteristics Required in Negatives for Albumen and Salted Paper Printing

Each photographic paper has a fixed set of tone reproduction characteristics; among these are the maximum density attainable on that paper, the number of tone steps of a graduated gray scale that it can reproduce (this is referred to as *scale length* or *gradation*) and the *contrast* of the paper, which refers to how rapidly or slowly the transitions from light to dark occur. In order to produce a negative with the proper contrast and density range to make the best possible print on albumen and salted papers, the tone reproduction characteristics of these papers will have to be taken into consideration.

Figure 33.

A special printing frame for "combination" printing, i.e., using several negatives in succession to make one print.

Unlike develop-out papers, where graded or variable-contrast materials offer a way to match the paper to the negative, consistently good results can only be obtained on albumen and salted papers by closely matching the negative to the requirements of the paper. Although there do exist some ways to affect print contrast with printing-out papers, these certainly do not provide as flexible a response to the negative as modern develop-out papers can. Also, many of the contrast-control techniques that are available for printing-out papers can only be used at the expense of optimum print quality.

Much experience has shown that even the densest and most contrasty negatives that will still print satisfactorily on develop-out papers do not possess sufficient density and contrast to make good prints on albumen and salted papers. To achieve the finest quality prints on either kind of paper—develop-out or printing-out—will mean exposing and processing negatives for that kind of paper alone, because "compromise" negatives will print well on neither kind. Even between albumen and the various kinds of salted papers significant differences in negative density range and contrast are called for. As a general rule, however, all printing-out papers require negatives with a greater density range—which implies higher maximum densities--than develop-out papers do.

EFFECT OF BINDER MATERIALS ON TONE REPRODUCTION

Guidance in producing suitable negatives for albumen and salted paper printing first comes from the nature of the binder material of the specific paper chosen. If the paper is glossy, as in the case of albumen paper, then a negative of shorter density range is required than would be necessary for a matte surfaced paper. In considering density range of a negative, it is the *difference* in density between the lowest and highest densities that needs to be determined, not just the highest density. A negative may be very dense indeed and still be "flat," with only a small relative difference between the minimum and maximum densities. The reason why glossy papers call for a negative with a lower density range is that glossy papers have a transparent binder (for example, albumen) which minimizes diffuse reflections and scattering of light by the paper fibers. This effectively produces more "brilliance" and contrast in the image by making the whites appear whiter and the shadow areas denser. The same amount of reduced silver which produces a deep shadow on glossy paper will produce a much paler looking shadow area on a matte surfaced print. To overcome this difficulty and produce a dense "black" on matte papers requires relatively more reduced silver, and that translates directly into longer exposure times. To permit longer exposure times a negative must have sufficient density in the highlights to keep the lighter tones in the print from becoming too dark. Hence a longer density range negative is called for with matte papers than with glossy papers. Following this rule, plain salted papers will require the greatest density range in a negative; matte papers like arrowroot and matte albumen, slightly less; and albumen paper still lower. Of course, the negative density range for albumen paper will still be considerably higher than that called for by develop-out papers.

USING A GRAY SCALE TO MEASURE
GRADATION AND CONTRAST

From the above explanation it will be clear that since there is a great deal of variation in the nature and amount of binder materials used on albumen and salted papers, no exact density ranges can be specified for all negatives intended for these different papers. However, there is a handy way to determine the necessary density range once a given paper has been fabricated. A sample sheet of paper is sensitized, printed from a 21-step gray scale and processed in the normal way for that paper. The exposure of the test sheet must be long enough so that the maximum possible density has been attained. This can be verified by making sure that the area of the print under the first step of the gray scale has reached the same density as the margins of the print which protrude beyond the gray scale itself. The number of steps of the gray scale which can be counted in the finished print is the "scale length" of that particular paper. Each photographic paper has its own characteristic number of steps produced in such a test. The appropriate negative density range for printing on that paper is approximately the same as the difference in density between the highest and lowest discernible steps on the gray scale. In practice, detail is always lost at the highest and lowest extremes of density in the print, so negatives with slightly shorter density ranges than those indicated by the test are usually employed. As would be expected, plain salted papers have the longest scale length in a test like this, matte papers have a slightly shorter one, and albumen paper the shortest.

Hübl found that in the tests he performed the scale length of glossy albumen paper was equal to that of platinum paper, and that the scale length of salted papers exceeded that of platinum paper by a considerable margin.[2] The long scale length of albumen and salted papers means that more of the detail present in negatives can be reproduced in the print than would be possible with shorter-scale materials, such as currently available develop-out papers. One of the reasons why all printing-out papers tend to have long scale lengths is because of the so-called "self-masking" property. This describes the phenomenon by which the density built up in shadow areas of the print during exposure acts as if it were a "mask" on the lowest density areas of the negative. As the silver builds up in the shadow areas of the print, it behaves as if it were additional density in the negative; this delays the attainment of maximum density in the print and tends to prevent the loss of all shadow detail before the highlight detail has time to "print in." The net effect of this "self-masking" action is to yield prints with good shadow density and detail while retaining a delicate gradation of lighter tones. With printing-out papers generally there is far less tendency to produce harsh "soot and chalk" prints than with developing-out papers.

Another important characteristic of every photographic paper that bears on the type of negative required for best results is its inherent contrast. As explained above, this refers to the progression of tones between the darkest and lightest, and whether this progression is smooth or abrupt. Two papers with the same scale length may not have the same contrast. For example, Hübl found in his investigations that although albumen and platinum paper possessed the same total scale length, when they were compared with the contrast of salted paper as reference, albumen paper had a slow progression of tones from the shadows to the middletones and a relatively abrupt jump from the middletones to white. With platinum paper the opposite takes place—the transitions from the highlights to the middletones are relatively soft while there is an abrupt jump down to the deep shadows.[3] These facts were ascertained by comparing the densities of each step of the gray scales on the three papers. The conclusions to be drawn from this are that although the density range of an optimum negative for albumen and platinum paper is the same, a negative intended for albumen printing should emphasize highlight detail at the expense of shadow detail, in order to compensate for relatively high contrast in the highlight end of the scale on albumen paper.

In performing similar tests, modern albumen and salted paper printers can measure print densities on a reflection densitometer and plot them graphically against the densities of the steps of the gray scale in order to get an accurate measurement of the gradation and contrast of the particular paper they are working with. Negative contrast can then be adjusted accordingly; however, the exposure and processing conditions for the test must be the same as those used in normal practice, or the test results will be misleading.

———————

Print Exposure

While print exposure may appear at first glance to be one of the more simple and straightforward aspects of albumen and salted paper printing, in reality it is one of the most complex. The biggest difficulty arises from the fact that the color and intensity of the exposing light affect the color and ultimate contrast of the print. Albumen and salted paper prints are primarily sensitive to ultraviolet radiation, and only to a much lesser extent to visible blue light. In choosing a light source to expose albumen and salted paper prints the main consideration is not how bright the light appears, but how much UV radiation it emits. The most convenient source of UV radiation is of course, the sun. Historically, no artificial light sources were available until the advent of the electric arc lamp in the 1880's, but the arc lamp was so impractical it was almost never used in the 19th century for printing purposes—it was dangerous and intimidating enough as a studio lighting device. The most satisfactory modern artificial light source is the metal halide lamp, developed in the 1960's and now used extensively in the graphic arts industry to expose lithographic plates and stencils for screen printing. Metal halide lamps exceed the sun in their UV output and do not have the drawback of releasing noxious fumes as did the carbon arc lamps that were previously used for those purposes. The disadvantage of metal halide lamps is their expense—a complete installation consists of a costly lamp tube, a lamp housing with a mechanical shutter and a separate power supply. Other, less expensive artificial light sources such as sunlamps, quartz halogen lamps, black-lite fluorescent tubes, or photofloods, are inadequate to the task.

For those without access to metal halide ramps the next best alternative is the sun. For all its problems and undependability, the use of sunlight (or more properly, daylight) has accounted for all but a tiny fraction of the albumen and salted paper prints ever made. The trouble with sunlight is that it is constantly changing in its UV output. The intensity of UV radiation in daylight waxes and wanes in annual and daily cycles, reaching a peak in the month of June in the annual cycle and at the hour of noon in the daily cycle. There is also the problem of an infinitely varying cloud cover. Still another difficulty associated with the use of daylight is the fact that the sensitivity of albumen and salted papers is considerably lowered when the temperature dips below 5° C, so printing outside in winter is practically impossible.

Figure 34.
An indoor printing studio,
ca. 1890. A south-facing
orientation was best
for printing.

EFFECT OF THE LIGHT SOURCE ON PRINT CONTRAST

A very intense light source lowers contrast in the print, while a weaker light tends to heighten print contrast slightly. Thus the old rule, found in many 19th-century manuals, which advises that dense, vigorous negatives be printed in sunlight and thin, weak negatives be printed in the shade. "Printed in shade" means facing open sky but not directly in sunlight. Also recommended in many old manuals is the technique of covering the printing frames with tissue paper or ground glass and printing in direct or filtered sunlight. Whether the majority of printing will be done in the shade or in sunlight depends on the character of the negatives to be printed. If the printer is using negatives of his or her own that were intended exclusively for albumen and salted paper printing—and providing the locale offers a fair amount of annual sunshine—then a good plan is to try and make the negatives so that they will stand up to full sunshine. Not only will the prints be more permanent, they will have a more pleasing tone and look richer and more brilliant.

The color of the exposing light also has an effect on print contrast. The higher the proportion of blue light and the lower the proportion of yellow light the exposure source contains, the greater will be the tendency toward a softer, flatter print. The greater the proportion of yellow and the less blue the exposing source contains, the greater will be the tendency toward a more contrasty print, but, of course, with an accompanying lengthening of exposure time.[4]

Figure 35.
A rack for holding
printing frames outdoors.
Such portable racks were
part of every small
studio's equipment.

EXPOSURE TIME

The "speed" of albumen and salted papers is exceedingly slow. Matte salted papers like arrowroot paper are the fastest, followed by plain salted papers and the slowest of the lot is albumen paper. An average exposure time of albumen paper in direct sunlight is 5 to 10 minutes, in shade, anywhere from ½ hour to several days. Of prime importance is the careful monitoring of exposure so that the correct amount of exposure is given the print; the necessary exposure required by a given negative will vary greatly with conditions. The exposure of albumen and salted paper prints must be carried on past the point where the print "looks right," since the prints lose density in the toning and fixing solutions. The degree of overprinting necessary depends on the nature of the binder material, the character of the negative and the type of toning bath used. Experience is the only way to know precisely how much overprinting is required, but a starting point for beginners might be to overprint one and a half "stops" for albumen paper and two "stops" for salted papers.

A good approach in determining the progress of exposure is to watch the margins of prints as they are exposing and make an initial check a short time after the margins appear to have reached maximum density. This advice would not apply in the case where a very thin negative is being printed because by the time the margins have attained maximum density, a print from a very thin negative will have most likely been spoiled. A guide to the point when maximum density has been attained is when the margins of the print begin to "bronze," that is, take on a greenish luster. At this point so much metallic silver has been reduced in the light-sensitive layer that a kind of saturation point is reached and particles of silver migrate to the surface of the layer and form a coherent, shiny film. If the "bronzing" has not progressed too far it may disappear during processing; otherwise, it will still be noticeable in the finished print, though not as prominently as before processing. Many old manuals on albumen printing recommend printing until the shadows are "just bronzed," and this is correct advice for many negatives, especially ones which can be printed in full sunshine.

Some Precautions in Printing

Neither the paper nor the printing frames should be excessively dry at the time of printing, because a certain amount of moisture is necessary in order to assure good sensitivity and contrast, especially with matte salted papers. The paper should contain enough moisture to be flexible and not feel dry and brittle. Conditioning the paper in a moist environment may be necessary. However, under no circumstances should the paper be damp or actually wet, because if some of the silver nitrate from the paper becomes transferred to the emulsion of the negative, red stains will result. Precautions against this accident should be taken whenever a valuable negative is to be printed. One mil (.001 inch) Mylar™ can be placed between the negative and the paper without sacrificing sharpness.

If a relatively cold printing frame is placed out in sunlight the expansion of the paper and the negative with heat may be unequal, and the result is a "doubled" image all around the outside edges of the image area while the center of the print remains sharp and crisp. This phenomenon is more likely to occur with large negatives and prints. Likewise, in bringing the frames inside to check the progress of exposure, care should be taken to avoid leaving half the frame lying open for more than the minimum time necessary to check exposure. Never open the frame to check exposure in sunlight or open shade; bring it inside to a safe location, preferably a room lit by a white incandescent light of low wattage. In this light the prints can be judged with reasonable leisure and safety.

A Note on Printing Historical Negatives

One of the pleasures of albumen and salted paper printing is to be able to print historical negatives on the kinds of positive printing materials for which many of these negatives were originally intended. A comparison between an albumen print made from a 19th-century negative and the "best possible" approximation of an albumen print made from the same negative on modern papers will quickly establish the superiority of the "real thing."

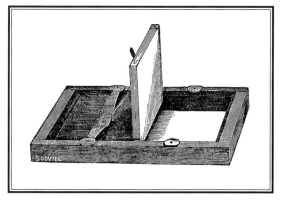

Figure 36.
A "Scovill" brand printing
frame. Usually made of
maple, such frames were
cheap and durable.

In printing from historical negatives the first and most important rule is to protect the negative; use the 1 mil Mylar™ spacer between the negative and the printing paper. Learn to handle glass negatives before attempting to print from a really valuable negative, because many negatives have been shattered in printing frames from too much pressure, or cracked by expansion in sunlight from an over-stressed frame. Use a frame that was intended for glass plates, and use a pad.

There is always some risk inherent in printing from a valuable negative, so the risk will have to be carefully weighed against the benefits of a facsimile print. For extremely valuable negatives a duplicate negative can be made at somewhat less risk to the original negative and prints then made from the duplicate negative. Whenever possible, this is the procedure that should be employed. Undoubtedly the making of new albumen prints from historical negatives will find a place in future photographic practice, because the appreciation of historical images is greatly enhanced by the use of the appropriate positive printing material. Any and all facsimile prints, however, should always be indelibly marked as such, with an embossed stamp or other method of identification.

CHAPTER 8

TONING

How simple this all is, the novice will exclaim; where are the difficulties of photographic printing? But stay, let us look at our print; we were very pleased with its tint when it came from the printing frame, but alas! the rich violet has given place [in the fixing bath] to a dull brick-red rusty colour, and our print is for that reason valueless.

—Fitt, 1856[1]

———————

Very early in the history of photographic papers the desire arose to modify the color and density of the images produced on printing-out papers. The effect of "hypo" on salted papers—however beneficial it might have been as a fixative—was to produce an unpleasant yellowish-brown image, and one that had suffered a serious loss in overall density as a result of the fixing process. Eventually a number of different approaches came to be used to intensify and modify the image color in albumen and salted papers. Many of these treatments had an effect on the permanence of the image as well as its appearance. The most important and significant to the lifespan of printing-out paper prints is the technique of noble-metal toning, in which the silver image is partially replaced by a deposit of metallic gold or platinum. This chapter presents the history of toning methods and the theory and practice of noble-metal toning.

History of Toning

HEAT TONING

Probably the oldest toning method was the use of heat to darken the image on salted papers. This method was used by Talbot and most other early printers; it no doubt evolved after a hot iron was applied to a finished print to flatten it, whereupon a distinct strengthening of image occurred. Heat toning with a hot iron must be carefully done in order to avoid scorching the paper, and the hot iron must never be applied to the face of the print. Recently a large number of Talbot's original negatives were printed on salted paper at the Kodak Museum in Harrow, England, and heat toning of the prints was accomplished by drying the prints in a modern heated print dryer.[2] Heat toning has more effect with plain salted papers and arrowroot paper than with other kinds of paper.

SULFUR TONING

The other type of toning used extensively in the first two decades of photography was sulfur toning. Known to photographers as the "old hypo" method, it involved the purposeful decomposition of the sodium thiosulfate fixing solution to the point where sulfur was set free to react with the silver image and form brownish silver sulfide, thus accomplishing a kind of toning. Presumably this effect was first noticed when fixing baths were allowed to become exhausted through continued use. To the surprise of photographers the older the fixing bath got, the more intense was the toning action. It soon became apparent, however, that prints fixed in a totally exhausted fixing bath speedily faded, sometimes within a few weeks. To overcome the difficulties of a completely exhausted fixing bath some photographers actually added old "hypo" to newly made up fixing solutions, in hopes of a compromise between toning and fixing. Some of the literature of the period 1840-1850 suggests that a fixing solution was ready only when it smelled of sulfur and the sides of the tray were encrusted with brown scum, or when the fixing solution itself had been black for several days!

Blanquart-Evrard suggested in 1847 that the "instant aging" of fixing solutions could be obtained by adding concentrated silver nitrate solutions.[3] An extension of the same idea was the addition of silver chloride, an ingredient called for in many early "toning-fixing" baths. The same liberation of sulfur from sodium thiosulfate could also be accomplished by acid additions to the fixing bath, and Blanquart-Evrard was also the first to propose the use of acetic acid additions to promote the toning effect.[4] Although the potentially dangerous effects of "old hypo" to the permanence of the prints (whether the hypo was truly "old" or artificially decomposed) were well known by 1850, the evidence against the practice was not totally conclusive. Even today many sulfur toned albumen and salted paper prints survive in good condition—for example many of the prints of Hill and Adamson. Apparently under some circumstances a stable image of silver sulfide could be produced by the sulfur toning methods used, though in general the odds in favor of permanence in the use of the practice were slim. One factor which undoubtedly helped was the recommendation made by many authors that "old hypo" be followed by a fresh, strong bath of "new hypo."

Gold Toning

The idea of gold toning paper prints was borrowed from daguerreotypists, who used a mixture of gold chloride and sodium thiosulfate called *sel d'or* (literally, salt of gold) to intensify and tone their daguerreotypes. This important modification of the original daguerreotype process was discovered in 1840 by the famous French physicist Hippolyte Fizeau, and it soon became standard practice.[5] Not until 1847 was the same idea applied to paper photographs; in that year P. F. Mathieu suggested the technique in a pamphlet entitled *Auto-Photographie*.[6] Unlike the enthusiastic adoption of "gilding" by daguerreotypists, gold toning of paper prints did not immediately catch on with photographers. Only when publicized after 1850 in the influential writings on photographic technique by Gustav LeGray did gold toning gain popularity, and then only slowly. LeGray was one of the best known and most successful photographers in France, and he did much to popularize all three of the great technical innovations in photography that appeared in the early 1850's—the wet collodion negative, the albumen print and gold toning of printing paper.

For a few years after 1850 the *sel d'or* method of gold toning was the most widely used for both albumen prints as well as salted papers. The effect of such a treatment was to change the image color from a yellowish-brown to either a cool brown, purple or bluish-black. The use of *sel d'or* constitutes what now would be called a toning-fixing bath. Since it is formed by mixing a solution of gold chloride into an excess of sodium thiosulfate ("hypo"), it retains its power to dissolve silver chloride and thus act as a fixing agent. It can also decompose and liberate sulfur if it is over-used or if it is made acidic by the introduction of acidic gold chloride. In fact, the usual practice of *sel d'or* toning involved a fairly good chance that sulfur toning and the release of potentially destructive invisible sulfur would take place before gold toning was fully accomplished. As in the case of the older sulfur toning approach, some *sel d'or* toned prints faded very quickly and others last to this day as vigorous as the day they were made. The difficulty with the method is that control over the outcome is impossible in the routine course of printing. In later years, during the era of emulsion-type printing-out papers (1890-1920), toning-fixing baths were reintroduced. Although more was known of the factors involved in assuring permanence, these new toning-fixing baths were also ultimately repudiated as too difficult to keep under control in the ordinary course of photographic printing.

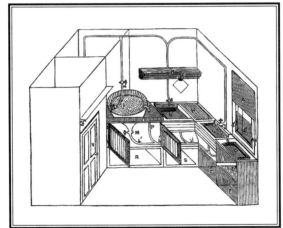

Figure 37.
"A silvering and toning room," Ca. 1875. Note the double door entrance arrangement.

The approach which came to be used in the late 1850's and which is known to be more favorable to permanence is called *separate* toning and fixing, in which the toning step precedes the fixing step and no thiosulfate is included in the toning formula. By 1860 the evidence against *sel d'or* toning was so conclusive that even its most obstinate adherents had to admit its inferiority.[7] A new and much more ef-

THE ALBUMEN & SALTED PAPER BOOK

fective method, called alkaline gold toning, had been proposed by James Waterhouse sometime around 1855.[8] This method called for separate toning and fixing, and the main innovation was the use of a toning bath composed of gold chloride and one or two mild alkalies. The alkaline solutions were found to be much more effective in their toning action and made rich browns and purple-browns easily attainable on albumen paper. The use of different combinations of alkaline substances with gold chloride produced different effects in toning, and the number of different formulae for toners quickly multiplied. Many 19th-century manuals contain 10 to 15 different formulae, most of them variations on the alkaline principle.

In 1867 another important class of gold toning baths was discovered, this time based on the combination of gold chloride with thiocyanates.[9] This type of toner achieves a more complete substitution of gold for silver and thus produces a colder image tone, generally deep purple tending to black. Thiocyanates are solvents of silver chloride, so when a print is introduced into a thiocyanate toner the image at first bleaches, then intensifies as the gold is deposited. More gold is consumed by thiocyanate toners than the alkaline varieties, and although they became fairly popular, they never eclipsed the alkaline toners so beloved by albumen printers. For the later emulsion-type gelatin and collodion printing-out papers, thiocyanate toners were particularly suitable, and became standard practice with these papers. Although thiocyanate (formerly called sulphocyanide in the old style chemical nomenclature) toners do dissolve silver chloride, they definitely are not a substitute for fixer, and subsequent fixation in sodium thiosulfate is still necessary.

Theory of Noble Metal Toning

Toning with noble metals confers two benefits on the albumen and salted paper printing processes. It improves the color and density of the image and it also provides a measure of protection against oxidation and sulfiding of the image silver by partially replacing and enclosing it with metallic gold or platinum. The reason why a toning step is necessary at all has to do with the physical characteristics of the silver image in printing-out papers. As discussed in Chapter 1, the image is composed of very small, very highly dispersed particles of metallic silver. Although metallic silver is considered to be fairly unreactive, it will still react with some substances, notably sulfur and oxidizing agents, especially when the silver is in a finely divided condition. The small particle size means that the silver has a very large surface area relative to its mass; hence a large portion of its total mass is on the surface and readily accessible to destructive chemical agents. Gold and platinum react much less readily with sulfur and are much more difficult to oxidize. A layer of gold or platinum on a silver particle will tend to shield the silver inside from attack, especially from oxidizing agents.

The factors which affect the ultimate color of a print are the size[10] and shape of the image particles, the distance between them[11] and the index of refraction of the medium in which they are dispersed.[12] In the toning process with noble metals the color of the image is modified by changing the size and shape of the silver particles through replacement of silver atoms by gold or platinum atoms. This enlargement of the metal aggregates which comprise the image causes the print to appear colder in tone, i.e., more neutral in color.

According to chemical theory it is only necessary to put a print into a solution which contains gold or platinum ions in order to have the substitution process take place. The rate of this substitution is greater for gold ions than platinum ions, although the rate may be modified by the presence of other substances in the toning solution.[13] Depending in part on whether the solution is acidic or alkaline, gold may take one of several ionic forms. In an acid toning bath such as a simple gold chloride solution, one atom of gold replaces three atoms of silver, a case in which toning action would lag far behind bleaching of the silver. The result would be a flat, lifeless image with a reddish color. In an alkaline toner the gold exists in a different ionic form and there is a more favorable substitution of one atom of gold for one atom of silver. Platinum toning, on the other hand, goes on much more effectively in an acid environment. In either gold or platinum toning, the substitution process creates silver chloride as a by-product. Toning must always be followed by a fixing step to remove this silver chloride.

The Practice of Gold Toning

CAUTION:
It is recommended that rubber gloves be
used during toning operations.

Toning is an inexact process. Standardized, repeatable results come only with experience and the attainment of repeatability in all other parts of the printing process. Among the factors which influence the outcome of the toning operation are the pH of the albumen or other binder materials used the pH of the silver solution the amount of silver deposited to form the image the thoroughness of the initial wash in processing the pH of the toning solution the presence of other substances in the toning solution the strength of the gold solution its temperature its age and the time of immersion of the print. Edward L. Wilson, one of the best known American writers on photography in the late 19th century, understated the case when he wrote, "The prints are not acted upon just alike."[14] For beginning printers a very helpful exercise in evaluating toning is to leave one or several prints completely untoned to form a basis of comparison with toned prints.

GOLD CHLORIDE
The main ingredient in all the gold toning formulae is gold chloride. The gold chloride which can be bought from photographic or chemical suppliers is always an acidic substance (technically called chlorauric acid), made by dissolving gold metal in a mixture of nitric and hydrochloric acids. True gold chloride is an unstable substance made by passing chlorine gas over gold leaf at elevated temperatures, and is not usually commercially available. Gold chloride of commerce is usually sold as either an amorphous orange mass or as a 1% solution in distilled water. Gold chloride in the dry state is sold in 15 grain (approx. 1 gram) amounts. Because the dry chemical is very deliquescent, it is packed in small hermetically sealed glass tubes.

Solutions of gold chloride are fairly stable if kept out of light and out of contact with organic materials. Stock solutions made up from the dry chemical should always be made with distilled water. A stock solution of 1% strength (one gram of the dry chemical to each 100 ml of water) is called for by most toner formulae. In the 19th century it was quite common for photographers to make their own gold chloride by dissolving gold coins in the mixed acids and then evaporating the solution to dryness or neutralizing the excess acid with chalk. Because of the fumes evolved and the dangers of the concentrated acids, this is not a recommended procedure for the home laboratory.

As stated earlier the pH of the toner solution has a definite effect on the toning process It is not clear whether or not it is simply pH difference of differences caused by the presence of other ions—or both—which account for the different results obtained by the numerous alkaline toning formulae found in the literature of albumen and salted paper printing A search of that literature reveals two different approaches to alkaline toning practice In the first approach the gold chloride stock solution is neutralized with calcium carbonate (i.e., chalk) before the toner is compounded. Calcium carbonate will not make the gold chloride alkaline, but will neutralize any free acid. In the other approach only the various alkaline substances called for in the toner formula are used to overcome the acidity of the gold stock solution.

For the modern practice of alkaline gold toning it is most convenient to use the gold stock solution in its acid condition, without pre-neutralizing it as much of the older literature recommends. Care must be taken, however, to see that approximately the same mildly alkaline condition is maintained in each batch of made-up toner. The stock gold solution retains a yellow color while still in the relatively inactive acidic state; when it has passed into the more active state through contact with alkaline substances, it becomes colorless. This decolorization is the best guide to the state of the toning bath. Some baths found in the older literature may take hours or even days to decolorize and become usable. The most common of these is the sodium acetate toner, which generally requires 24 hours to "ripen" before it can be used. The printer who wishes to standardize the toning process as much as possible can monitor the pH of the toning solution, but for most applications sufficient control is obtainable simply by making up the toner according to a proven formula and visually observing the progress of toning.

The toning solution should not be made too alkaline because although it tones more quickly in that condition, it also loses its activity much more rapidly. Too active toners, whether from too much gold content or too high pH, do not produce pleasant tones and are more difficult to control. A leisurely pace in toning allows each print to receive individual attention. Making the toner too alkaline will result in baths that still contain a great deal of gold but no longer will tone prints. Most alkaline baths are intended for "one-use" toning, and be-

THE ALBUMEN & SALTED PAPER BOOK

come inactive spontaneously after a few hours. There is no clue other than the cessation of toning action to indicate the point at which a toning bath has become inactive or exhausted. Baths made with sodium acetate can be used repeatedly if strengthened with additions of gold stock solution.

STRENGTH OF GOLD TONING SOLUTIONS

Papers with porous surfaces, such as arrowroot, plain salted paper, etc., require toners with much less gold content than those intended for glossy albumen paper. These porous papers tone more quickly, and would rapidly become overtoned in the strong baths employed for albumen paper. Toning baths for matte salted papers should contain .1 to .2 g gold chloride per liter of toning solution, while glossy albumen paper toners should contain between .4 and .5 g gold chloride per liter of toning solution. Toning of both albumen and salted papers is generally done by inspection, and should take from 3 to 15 minutes depending on conditions and the kind of paper being toned. Toning should generally be carried on well past the point when a visible change takes place in the image color. The toning solution should be used at temperatures of 17-20°C, and prints require constant agitation in the toning solution. The toner solution is ruined by even a trace of fixer, so cleanliness and care are requited. The toning operation is best carried on in weak incandescent light so that the color of the prints may be accurately determined. In the case of glossy albumen paper the toning should be continued until only the shadows of the print retain their original warm color by transmitted light. Judging toning by looking at prints lying flat in a tray may be deceptive. After toning is completed the prints should be placed in running water and given a 5-minute wash before fixing them.

GOLD TONER FORMULAE

The following are alkaline gold toning formulae:

BORAX BATH

BORAX (SODIUM BORATE)	10 g
1% GOLD CHLORIDE SOLUTION	40 ml
WATER	TO MAKE 1 liter

SODIUM ACETATE BATH

FUSED SODIUM ACETATE	20 g
1% GOLD CHLORIDE SOLUTION	40-50 ml
WATER	TO MAKE 1 liter

The following is a thiocyanate-based toner:

THIOCYANATE TONER

SODIUM THIOCYANATE	15-20 g
1% GOLD CHLORIDE SOLUTION	60-80 ml
WATER	TO MAKE 1 liter

Platinum Toning

HISTORY OF PLATINUM TONING

The first published mention of platinum toning occurred in 1856, when a photographer in Istanbul, M. De Caranza, recommended toning photographs with an acidified platinic chloride solution.[15] Very little notice was taken of De Caranza's suggestion because such a toner has only a very slight toning action and possesses a strong tendency to bleach the silver image. In fact all platinic chloride formulae have so little toning energy that at their best they are restricted to use with matte papers, and are totally ineffective with albumen paper. On the other hand, the platinous chloride salts, chiefly potassium chloroplatinite, are very active toners when combined with acids,[16] and have a smaller tendency to attack the silver image.

Potassium chloroplatinite was a fairly obscure substance certainly not one generally available to photographers—until 1879, the year in which Willis began to market the platinotype process. In this process potassium chloroplatinite is an indispensable ingredient. Many workers of the platinotype process also used silver papers, and in 1886 J. Reynolds discovered that potassium chloroplatinite was a very energetic toner of silver prints,[17] yielding brown and brownish-black tones instead of the purplish and bluish-black tones obtained with gold toners. In 1889 Alfred Stieglitz also published one of the pioneering platinum toner formulae for silver papers, consisting simply of nitric acid, potassium chloroplatinite and water.[18]

Platinum toning of silver prints became quite a popular practice, especially with matte-surfaced papers. Its most widespread use occurred during the period 1895-1925 when matte collodion and matte gelatin emulsion type printing-out papers were so popular. Matte gelatin papers were often toned only with platinum and therefore have a brown hue, while matte collodion papers were generally toned with both gold and platinum. This produced the familiar olive-black color so often seen in the studio portraits of the era 1895-1920. Platinum toning was also preferred for the various salted papers in use during this time, such as the many kinds of arrowroot and matte albumen paper.

THE PRACTICE OF PLATINUM TONING

The effects obtainable with platinum toning do seem to harmonize especially well with a matte surface, although platinum toning can be used with albumen and other kinds of glossy paper. The main technical difference between gold and platinum toning is that gold toning goes on best in an alkaline environment, while platinum toning requires a neutral or acidic condition. One difficulty in platinum toning is the tendency to produce yellowish highlights if the toning is carried on too long, or if the solution is too strong or too acidic. Another is the tendency of any impurities such as silver nitrate or sodium thiosulfate to rob the toning bath of its activity by altering the platinum to an irreducible condition. For this reason prints to be toned in a platinum toner must be well washed and treated in a 5% sodium chloride solution for 2 minutes and then washed again for 5 minutes in running water before being placed in the toning solution. Still another precaution to be observed is to wash the prints *well* after toning, to be sure that none of the acidic platinum toner is carried into the fixing bath.

A useful platinum toning formula is as follows:

POTASSIUM CHLOROPLATINITE, 1% SOL	50 ml
CITRIC ACID	4 g
WATER	750 ml

Combined gold and platinum toning may be used to obtain neutral blacks; tone the prints in the Borax gold bath until they are lilac in color, and long enough in the platinum toner to achieve a neutral color. It is not possible to consistently attain the absolutely neutral black characteristic of the platinum print itself, however.

CHAPTER 9

FIXATION AND WASHING

The permanence of prints on albumenised paper and their freedom from yellowness with age undoubtedly depend on the elimination, by the fixing bath, of the insoluble salts of silver.

—A. Haddon and F.B. Grundy, July, 1897[1]

This chapter deals with two important operations in the processing of albumen and salted papers. The first is the fixing step, in which the unexposed light-sensitive substances are removed from the prints by treatment in a solution of sodium thiosulfate. The second and equally important step is the washing out of the chemical products of the fixation process. These must be removed because they are unstable and will cause yellowing and fading of the image if allowed to remain. Washing prints in running water and treatment in a "washing aid" such as a 1% sodium sulfite solution or Kodak Hypo Clearing Agent™ are the means employed to remove the by-products of fixation.

While the broad outlines of the fixing and washing operations with albumen and salted papers are similar to those of other photographic materials, there are some significant differences. Because of the extremely small size of the silver image particles in these papers, the image is considerably more vulnerable to chemical attack, especially from the residual products of fixation. Therefore it cannot be over-stressed that strict adherence to correct procedures in fixing and washing is the only way to assure optimum permanence in albumen and salted paper prints.

Theory of the Fixation Process

In an exposed but unprocessed print the image layer consists of the metallic silver image itself, the binder material used (starch, gelatin, albumen, etc.) and unexposed light-sensitive silver salts. These are primarily silver chloride, but depending on whatever additions have been made to the salting or sensitizing solutions, silver citrate, silver chromate or other silver salts may be present. In order to render the image stable the light-sensitive substances must be removed, ideally leaving behind only the binder material and a silver (and gold or platinum, if the print has been toned) image.

Silver chloride and the other silver salts are not soluble in water; they can only be removed through a chemical reaction with another substance, in which a new water-soluble "complex" is formed. The choice of fixers or more properly, "complexing agents" for silver salts—is somewhat limited. Among the substances which have some fixing or stabilizing action are ammonia, potassium cyanide, strong chloride solutions, thiocyanates, thiourea, sodium sulfite and sodium and ammonium thiosulfate. Of all these sodium thiosulfate has the fewest drawbacks for the purpose of fixing silver printing-out papers, and it has been in almost exclusive use for that task since the very earliest days of photography.

HISTORY OF FIXATION WITH THIOSULFATES
The discovery of the fixative properties of sodium thiosulfate (or "hyposulfite of soda" as it was known then) was made in 1839 by Sir John F. W. Herschel. He had heard that both Talbot and Daguerre had evolved photographic processes, and decided to make some investigations himself. He first applied sodium thiosulfate for the purpose of fixing silver chloride papers on January 29, 1839. The idea came to him because of some observations he had made in the years 1819 and 1820, when he discovered the substance sodium thiosulfate and noticed that it was a solvent for silver chloride.[2] A short while later he communicated his epochal discovery to Talbot, who up to this point had not been truly fixing but merely "stabilizing" with a strong solution of sodium chloride. Talbot at first disdained "hypo," but later incorporated it into his own process, as did Daguerre, who had also been "stabilizing" with a strong sodium chloride solution (in a stabilizing treatment the silver chloride is not removed, it is merely changed into a less sensitive form).

Sodium thiosulfate in its pentahydrate form has the chemical formula $Na_2S_2O_3 \cdot 5H_2O$. Each thiosulfate ion contains 2 atoms of sulfur, and it is chiefly the presence of sulfur that necessitates the removal of the silver thiosulfate complexes which are the products of the fixation process. Also, any thiosulfate which has not "complexed" with silver must be removed as well, because the thiosulfate ion is itself unstable and can be easily decomposed, thus releasing elemental sulfur to attack the silver image. However, in dry crystalline form sodium thiosulfate is a stable substance, although it should be kept in a tightly stoppered bottle. When dissolved in water, sodium thiosulfate is not stable, and after a time partially decomposes to sodium sulfite and elemental sulfur. For this reason fixing solutions intended for use with albumen and salted paper prints should not be made in advance; the fixer solution should preferably be made up just prior to use, so that spontaneous decomposition of the thiosulfate is kept to a minimum.

CHEMICAL REACTIONS INVOLVED IN FIXATION

The actual reactions involved in the fixing process are fairly complicated, and there are probably at least three different kinds of silver-thiosulfate complexes formed during fixation.[3] Studies of these reactions have led to the conclusion that certain conditions must prevail for the most effective fixation as well as for the most complete removal of free thiosulfate and silver-thiosulfate complexes. The most important of these conditions is that thiosulfate ions must be present in excess. There must be more thiosulfate ions present than are needed to react with all the silver ions present, or else insoluble complexes are formed which cannot be washed from the image layer.[4] Another way of stating this is that one of the complexes formed during fixation is only soluble in fresh thiosulfate.

In practice this means that two fixing baths are necessary; the first one does the bulk of the "complexing," while the second insures that the complexes ultimately formed can be washed out of the print. It is apparent from this why only fresh fixer solutions are likely to result in optimum print permanence. As the fixer solution approaches a point of exhaustion, it loses its ability to form soluble silver-thiosulfate complexes. Studies have also shown that the fixing process is completed fairly rapidly, and prolonged fixation is much more injurious to prints than is generally believed. Fixing too long will allow thiosulfate to penetrate inside the paper fibers, in which case it becomes almost impossible to remove.

Another potential difficulty arises from the pH of the fixing bath.

Although modern gelatin-based photographic materials are generally fixed in an acid hardening type of fixing bath, albumen and salted paper prints are best fixed in an *alkaline* solution of sodium thiosulfate to which no hardeners have been added. Alkaline thiosulfate solutions are necessary for two reasons: first, the slight alkalinity prevents any acids which might be inadvertently introduced into the fixing bath from decomposing the sodium thiosulfate and liberating sulfur. Second, an acid fixing bath would tend to attack the finely divided metallic silver of the image, causing excessive bleaching of the highlights and middletones in the print. This attack on the image silver itself is minimized when the pH of the fixer is kept on the alkaline side.

The Practice of Fixation

Based on the theoretical considerations given above, fixation of albumen and salted papers is best done in a freshly made-up solution composed as follows:

SODIUM THIOSULFATE (PENTAHYDRATE)	150 g
SODIUM CARBONATE	2 g
WATER	TO MAKE 1 liter

The fixing bath should be made with water slightly warmer than the desired working temperature of 18 to 20° C, since some heat is always consumed in the formation of the solution. It is important that the fixing bath not be too cold, since too great a temperature differential between the fixing bath and the other processing solutions might cause blistering of albumen paper. To insure that fixation is properly carried out, the prints must be washed free of other substances—especially acidic platinum toning baths—before they are placed in the fixer. Two separate trays of fresh fixer are required. The prints are placed in the first fixing bath and agitated constantly for 4 minutes, drained for at least 5 seconds, then placed in the second fixing bath and agitated constantly for another 4 minutes. It is important that there be enough fixing solution in each tray to easily accommodate the number of prints being fixed at one time, and that care be taken to see that the whole surface of each print is constantly washed over with fixer solution. As indicated in Chapter 3, this fixing procedure is applicable to all silver printing-out papers.

FIXER EXHAUSTION

It is difficult to establish the point at which a fixing bath becomes exhausted. The value of maximum solubility of silver chloride in sodium thiosulfate is known, but that does not help to establish the practical limits of use for a fixing bath, since the presence of excess thiosulfate is required to insure maximum permanence. Estimates in the literature suggest that no more than 150 8 x 10 inch prints should be fixed in 1 liter of 15% sodium thiosulfate solution,[5] but it seems that a much more conservative estimate should be made when optimum permanence is desired. To assure the longest life for a print, probably no more than 10 to 15 prints (approximately 8 x 10 inches in size) should be fixed in each liter of fixer solution.

The silver content of printing-out papers is very high relative to conventional develop-out materials, and it can also vary from one kind of albumen or salted paper to another. The relatively high silver content and the vulnerability of the colloidal silver image are the reasons why such a conservative estimate of fixer exhaustion is necessary. Compared to the other costs of albumen and salted paper printing, the price of fixer is cheap, and frequent renewal of the fixing bath is a worthwhile investment which helps insure durability of the finished prints.

COLOR CHANGES DURING FIXATION

During fixation the prints undergo a dramatic change in color, in which the original brilliant purple or brown color is transformed into a much yellower and duller brown hue, accompanied at the same time by a loss of density. The reasons for this color and density change—a characteristic phenomenon in all silver printing-out papers—have to do with the physical structure of the metallic silver which forms the image. In an exposed but unfixed print the silver image particles exist in a highly dispersed state, forming a kind of "solid solution" of metallic silver in silver chloride.[6] The color and density of this system is determined by the size and amount of metallic particles as well as the combined refractive indices of silver chloride and whatever binder materials have been used on the paper.

Upon fixation the silver chloride is removed and the metallic silver particles undergo a "packing" process and accumulate into aggregates of particles.[7] At the same time the refractive index of the system is lowered by the removal of the silver chloride. Together these physical and chemical changes cause a loss of particle covering power i.e., print density and shift the color of the print toward yellow. In fact, any physical change in the image layer causes a shift of print color. A good example of this is the reddening of prints that occurs when they are placed in the initial wash water; swelling of the image layer is the actual cause of the color shift. When prints dry they undergo another change, becoming more neutral in color and gaining slightly in density as the image layer contracts.

Washing of Prints

GENERAL CONSIDERATIONS

The purpose of washing is to remove the sodium thiosulfate and silver thiosulfate complexes that remain in the print after fixation. Over the years a great deal of attention has been paid to the theory and practice of washing photographic materials, but insufficient washing still remains a leading cause of the deterioration of photographs. The washing of photographic prints is more difficult than the washing of films, primarily because of the absorption of thiosulfate into the paper fibers. With prints the rate of washing slows down tremendously at the lower levels of thiosulfate concentration,[8] and in practice it is impossible to remove every trace of thiosulfate simply by washing in water.

In the case of albumen and salted papers, effective washing is even more important than in modern photographic materials. In the older papers, the silver image is in much more intimate contact with the paper fibers than is the case with modern papers, where a substratum of baryta and gelatin (or polyethylene) separates the image layer from the paper base. Therefore, with albumen and salted papers a combination of both proper fixation and effective washing is necessary to insure that the base paper does not become a reservoir of image-threatening substances. It is very important in this regard that immersion of the prints in the fixing solution is not prolonged beyond the recommended time. Experimental evidence on the washing of albumen and salted paper prints is almost nonexistent. However, the factors which affect the rate of washing gelatin prints are probably valid for these papers as well.

WASHING AIDS

The removal of thiosulfate from prints cannot be accomplished simply by washing in water, if a print of optimum stability is desired. In fact, water is such a poor remover of low levels of thiosulfate from prints that an extra step in processing is needed to assure maximum print permanence. This consists of treating the prints in a so-called "washing aid" or hypo clearing agent in order to facilitate more complete removal of the thiosulfate. These treatments are effective because they displace the absorbed thiosulfate ions and replace them with less harmful and more soluble ions of various salts. The best "washing aid" for albumen and salted papers consists of a 1% solution of sodium sulfite, although proprietary formulas such as Kodak Hypo Clearing Agent™ may also be used.

Figure 38.

A semi-automatic print washer and agitator, ca. 1890.

WASHING CONDITIONS AND APPARATUS

The actual apparatus and conditions of washing are very important to the efficiency of the washing process. In general the desirable factors in the design of washing apparatus are assurances that sufficient flow of water covers the entire print surface, and that the entire volume of water is changed at least every 5 minutes. The temperature of the wash water should remain fairly constant at approximately the same temperature as the other processing solutions. Where the design of the washing system is less than perfect—for example when more than 2 prints are washing in a tray equipped with a tray siphon—hand agitation of the prints is absolutely necessary. Another common washing apparatus is merely a round tub with a water inlet that forces the prints to swirl in a circle. This kind of washing appara-

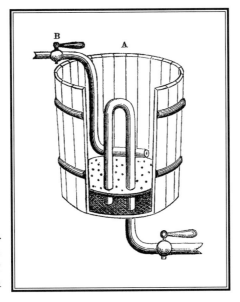

Figure 39.
A print washing tank with
a circular water flow and
siphon drain, ca. 1870.

tus also demands frequent hand agitation to insure proper washing. Certainly the average conditions for washing prints in the 19th century were less than optimum. Often the prints were washed in ice cold water, or without the benefits of running water of any kind. The basic technique recommended in many manuals of the time was to remove the prints from the wash tray, squeegee them, then return them to a fresh tray of water and agitate them. This procedure was to be repeated over a period of time that ranged from 12 hours (according to Abney)[9] to only 15 minutes (according to Haddon and Grundy).[10] Nineteenth-century photographers were very much concerned with assuring removal of thiosulfate, and then as now, there were all sorts of washing devices and hypo-elimination preparations on the market.

WASHING TIME

The washing time of prints depends on the thickness of the paper base and the nature of the binder material used. Generally, the thicker the base paper, the longer the wash time required, and also the longer the treatment time required for the "washing aid." The removal of thiosulfate is also affected by the diffusion rate of substances through the image layer, so that albumen paper will probably require substantially longer to wash than papers like arrowroot or plain salted paper that possess more porous image layers. The wash times recommended below are intended to be safe for glossy albumen paper and all other salted papers as well. Some papers, however, may be injured by prolonged washing—the image layer may begin to dissolve—in which case a shorter wash time is indicated.

METHOD FOR WASHING ALBUMEN
AND SALTED PAPERS

After fixing is complete the prints should be given a short (2 to 4 minute) wash in running water before treatment in the "washing aid." This water wash removes the vast bulk of the thiosulfate and avoids overloading the mechanism of ion-exchange in the sodium sulfite solution to follow. The prints are then to be treated for 3 to 4 minutes with constant agitation in the following solution:

SODIUM SULFITE (ANHYDROUS)	10 g
WATER	TO MAKE 1 liter

This constitutes a 1% solution. It should be used only once and discarded. The solution may be made in advance. The rate of exhaustion for this solution is the same as that of the fixer solution—no more than 20 prints, approximately 8 x 10 inches, should be treated in 1 liter of solution.

Following the sodium sulfite bath the prints should receive 30 minutes of washing in running water in an effective print washer. Extremely heavy base stocks and very thick coatings of albumen may indicate that a longer wash time—40 to 50 minutes—is required.

Figure 40.
A drying rack for prints.
The prints were not
allowed to become truly
dry, but were mounted
while still damp.

Drying the Prints

After the wash step is completed, the prints should be removed from the print washer and either gently squeegeed, face-down on clean glass, or blotted with photographic quality blotters to remove excess water. They should then be air dried face-up on clean fiberglass screens or on suitable blotters. The degree of curling in the dried prints depends on the thickness of the paper base and the nature of the binder material used. Thin papers coated with heavy layers of albumen tend to curl the most—hence the almost universal historical practice of mounting albumen prints while still damp. Prints may be dried under weights or in a book press to help prevent curling; in this case the coated side of the print should be against silicone release paper, while blotters should be placed against the back side of the print.

CHAPTER 10

FINISHING, MOUNTING
AND STORAGE

*"If we find that a little sour paste is quite sufficient to injure the picture,
it is no satisfaction to us to be told that it consists of metallic silver, one
of the most indestructible of metals."*

—T.F. Hardwich, May, 1856[1]

O nce the prints have been washed and dried, they require further handling before they can be displayed or stored in the
safest and most advantageous way. The choice of finishing materials and treatments bears directly on both the attractiveness and
permanence of albumen and salted papers. Proper storage is also
essential to optimum permanence in any photographic material.
This chapter presents a recommended contemporary approach to
the finishing and storage of albumen and salted papers, together
with some historical notes on 19th-century practice.

Figure 41.
Carte de visite albums,
ca. 1870. At right is a
stereo viewer.

Preparing Prints for Display or Storage

The characteristics of the prints themselves will determine the most suitable method to prepare them for storage or display. Depending on the thickness of the rawstock and the type of organic binder on the print surface, most prints will need some type of flattening treatment after drying. The most common method is to place them between acid-free blotters under weights, or in a book press. This process should be undertaken when the prints are slightly damp or at least not when they are bone-dry, and above all it requires patience. Do not try to hasten the process with excessive pressure, although a fair amount of pressure is needed to accomplish the flattening.

The use of heat in the process of drying or flattening may alter the appearance of some types of salted papers, especially plain salted papers. Upon heating the prints turn colder in image color and become somewhat darker. This technique was actually a part of the process that Fox Talbot used in the production of his prints. The last step in finishing his prints was to go over them with a hot iron to "intensify" them. Drying salted paper prints in a heated drum type of dryer may similarly change them.

Ideally, once the prints are flattened they can be placed in a sleeve or mat without a mounting process of any kind. Most salted papers, because they are made on relatively heavy paper and do not have a great deal of binder material on their surface, can be simply matted and do not require mounting. Mounting is a process that should be employed only when necessary, and not as a matter of course. Unfortunately, the thinner papers used in albumen printing and the tendency to curl imparted by heavy layers of albumen will often necessitate that prints be flattened by mounting them onto a suitable material.

History of the Finishing and Mounting of Albumen Prints

A look at the 19th-century approach to the finishing of albumen prints is instructive, because it relates quite closely to modern practice. It is rare to encounter 19th century albumen prints that have not been mounted onto some kind of cardboard mount. The main reason for this is the fact that the thin paper stock used for albumen printing cannot resist the tendency to curl of the layer of albumen itself. The force exerted by a thick layer of albumen is quite enough, if a print has been incorrectly mounted, to tear the print in half; the impossibility of getting such a print to lie flat of its own accord is obvious. Even if a window mat is used to keep an un-mounted albumen print relatively flat, most prints have undesirable ridges, creases and "bumps" in the print surface that catch the light and detract from the image.

Figure 42.

Trimming prints using a rotary blade trimming knife and brass templates. A rotary knife made it easier to follow the outlines of curved templates.

The process of mounting an albumen print helps to impart more depth and contrast to the image, and creates a smooth, level surface which can be viewed from different angles without the interference of these uneven surface reflections. In the 19th century the prints were mounted when damp, and if they had become dry, they were rewetted and blotted before mounting was attempted.[2] The modern mounting method given below also adopts this precaution.

MOUNTING ADHESIVES USED IN THE 19th CENTURY
The adhesive used for mounting albumen prints was usually starch, although gelatin[3], gum arabic[4], dextrine[5] and albumen itself[6] were

Higgins' Photo Mounter.

THE

NEW ADHESIVE

FOR

Mounting

Photographs,

ETC.

A Novel and Superior [...]
prepared for Mounting Pho[...]
totypes, Engravings, Scrap[...]
WARRANTED TO KEEP CORR[...]
NOTHING INJUR OUS SO AND MOUNT [...]
ANS IN WIND RECORE MUSIC 12 MART [...]
WANAR.
3-oz. Jars, 15c.   6-oz. Jars, 25[...]

Figure 43.
Advertisement for
Higgins' Photo Mounting
Paste, 1894, described by
the manufacturer as "not
a starch or flour paste,
but a vegetable glue."

also used. Sometimes starch and gelatin were mixed together.[7] Photographic conservators faced with the problem of removing albumen prints from their mounts agree that pure fresh starch has proven itself as the best choice for a mountant; it is removable with the least difficulty and has not attacked the prints. Ordinary "glue"—which is an impure form of gelatin—was known to be a cause of trouble even in the 1850's, but it was used as an expedient, along with many other destructive substances such as rancid flour paste and India rubber solution.

The mounting boards used in the 19th century were a constant source of potential danger for the photographic image. A typical 19th-century mount was composed of a thin top and bottom sheet of relatively good quality paper, with a center filler of poor quality pulp board. This pulp center was often loaded with lignin, the noncellulose component of wood, whose presence leads to the acidification of the entire mount and eventually of the photographic print itself. The most common problems seen today that result from poor quality mount boards are brittleness and yellowing in the print caused by acidification of the mounting cardboard, and the brownish-red flecks and stains known as "foxing." This "foxing" may be the result of mold and fungus growth, or may also be caused by the presence of metallic salts in the mount board.[8]

Staining from decomposed mounting adhesives is also common, either initiated or compounded by the acidification of the mount board. Today, many albumen prints are in desperate need of separation from their original mount and re-mounting on a more durable and less dangerous material. Danger from the mount board is especially acute for albumen prints because they were made on such thin rawstock—very little barrier exists between the silver image and the potentially destructive substances in the mount. Attempting to forestall further damage to albumen prints from defective mounts and mountants is one of the single largest tasks in photographic conservation, and is among the most commonly requested procedures in the conservation of photographic prints.

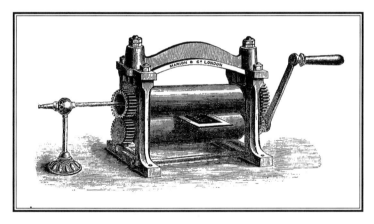

Figure 44.
"Marion's Self-adjusting Rolling Press & Burnisher," 1884. Note the gas tube in the upper roller.

Fortunately albumen is a very durable substance, and can usually withstand the rigors of unmounting and remounting. More trained and experienced photographic conservators are needed for this task if our photographic heritage—historical as well as aesthetic—is to be preserved.

ROLLING MACHINES AND BURNISHERS

In addition to curling the paper, sometimes heavy layers of albumen can have a horny, rough surface that may obscure the finest details. Rolling and smoothing the prints in a press or roller device tends to restore some of the detail and also provides a glossier surface and increased contrast. For this reason, and also to improve adhesion of the print to the mount, albumen prints were routinely subjected to a process of rolling and smoothing after mounting.

There were several styles of rolling machines used in the 19th century, but all of them accomplished the same purpose of making the prints glossier and smoother. Small prints—especially "cabinet" size portraits and stereo views—were often given an extra glossy finish in a heated roller device called a "burnisher." In skilled hands a burnisher could produce a mirror-like gloss on albumen prints. The operators of portrait studios in the 1880's and 90's sometimes ballyhooed the gloss of their prints by giving them fantastic names like "French Enamel" and "Extra Superior Finish."

Figure 45.
A flat-bed type of
rolling press, of English
manufacture.

Some types of rolling machines were similar to wringers on old-style washing machines. One roller was smooth and did the work of polishing the print while the other roller sometimes had ribbing to bite into the mount and propel the print through the machine. Many small photographic prints of the period 1875-1890—landscapes, portraits and stereo views—have cross-hatched indentations on the back of the mount. Such prints were rolled in a wringer-type rolling machine with a ribbed drive roller. In other cases the back side of the print mounts will simply be noticeably shiny with a "squeezed" appearance; this is evidence of having been rolled in a flat-bed or smooth-roller type machine. Flat-bed style machines resembled a copperplate etching press and could be used with either mounted or unmounted prints. The prints were placed face down on the steel bed of the press and a large roller applied pressure to the back.

A Contemporary Approach to Finishing, Display, and Storage

The object of finishing (and mounting, if necessary) is to present and store prints in the safest and most attractive way. A simple, direct approach is to place prints in individual transparent polyester sleeves, together with a piece of two-ply, acid-free rag board to impart rigidity and prevent creasing of the print during handling. These are available in most of the common photographic sizes, and are a satisfactory way to store and examine prints with a minimum of wear and tear. Any cataloging or identifying information that is to be placed directly on the print should be lightly written on the back of the print in pencil, and as close to the edge as possible. These polyester (also called Mylar™) sleeves will not damage the prints at normal humidities and temperatures, and at the present time do appear safe for long-term storage.

MATTING PRINTS

For prints that merit more attractive presentation or more protection in storage, a window mat is the preferred method. A window mat is two superimposed pieces of very high quality cardboard that are hinged together along one edge. The print lies between the two pieces of board and is visible through a hole—called the "window"—cut in the top piece of the board. Window mats should be made from what is commonly called "museum board," which means that it is composed of 100% cellulose fiber and is acid-free. Although several other kinds and grades of mat boards are available, it is best to select only those materials that will lead to optimum permanence. In choosing mat board for use with albumen and salted paper prints, most museums choose a cream or ivory-tinted board, in order to harmonize with the warm colors of print-out silver images. The hinges of the mats should be made of linen treated on one side with a special acid-free, water-soluble adhesive.

The "mat," as it is usually called, fits into a frame as a unit when a print is to be framed. The "window" of the mat is cut with a special beveled cutter so that it does not cast a shadow onto the edge of the print. If a print is to be stored in a window mat, a piece of acid-free paper or polyester sheeting is placed on top of the print (under the window) in order to protect the print from dust and mechanical damage. These two methods—transparent sleeves and window mats—are the most common approaches to presentation and storage used in photographic collections at the present time.

One advantage of both the sleeve and the window mat are that they form a safe environment for the print yet are not permanently attached to it. In the case of the window mat, there are two approaches to holding the print in position under the "window" of the mat. The first is to use what are called mounting corners, which are hollow folded paper triangles made from acid-free paper. The corners are held in place by the same kind of linen tape that forms the hinge of the mat. To use mounting corners, the four corners of the print are inserted into the folded triangles, the print is positioned under the "window," and finally the paper triangles are adhered to the bottom piece of the mat.

HINGING PRINTS

If the print has no borders and is all image area, another approach is necessary. This alternative method involves the use of "hinges," which are slips of very thin Japanese paper that are adhered along one edge of the print and then adhered to the bottom board of the window mat after the print has been correctly positioned. The adhesive for this purpose should always be a specially prepared paste of wheat or rice starch. The method of preparing this paste will be detailed later on in this chapter. The actual Japanese paper hinges should be about 2 inches long and 1 inch wide; two of them are usually needed. The hinges should be cut from the sheets of Japanese paper by tearing along a straight edge, and not by cutting with a scissors, because in this way the fibers taper smoothly off and there is less chance of the hinges showing through a print on thin paper. Just a small portion of the narrow dimension of the hinge need protrude onto the back of the print itself. The goal in the use of hinges (as in *all* conservation treatments) is to make them as reversible— that is, removable without trace or damage to the print—as possible and still have them perform the task of holding the print in position. Longer hinges than necessary are sometimes used so that if the print requires re-matting, the hinge may be simply cut off with enough of the hinge remaining to reattach the print in another mat.

A Conservator's Mounting Method

The following is a very satisfactory method of mounting albumen and other sorts of photographic prints. It is useful for both modern albumen prints and 19th-century prints that have been removed from their original mounts and are in need of remounting. This method was worked out by David E. Kolody, a photographic conservator in Boston, Massachusetts, and it appears here through his courtesy.

Although more complicated than other mounting methods, this method has several advantages: first, it adheres the print to the support in such a way that an absolutely flat and smooth surface is created. This is important because it most closely approximates the surface quality of the print on its original mount. Albumen prints are generally most effective when their surface is absolutely flat and smooth. Remarkably, albumen prints mounted by Kolody's method retain a "rolled" appearance on their new support, even though no high-pressure rolling press is employed in the mounting procedure. Second, this method is equally effective with large or small prints. It allows 18 x 24 inch prints to be mounted almost as easily as 8 x 10's. These large prints, by no means uncommon, are notoriously difficult to work with. Third, the method is easily reversible without resorting to strong solvents, and does not permanently attach the print to its mount. Fourth, no heat is required and there is no danger of altering the color of a print or otherwise damaging it with heat. Dry mounting (in the modern sense) should never be used with albumen or salted paper prints, because of color shifts caused by heat, and the irreversibility of the process.

SUMMARY OF THE MOUNTING PROCEDURE

The basic principle of this mounting method is to provide a rigid temporary support of Plexiglas™ on which the print is mounted and dried, so that the print is held flat until it has become completely dry and its internal forces have equalized out. Of course, if the print and its mount were simply pasted down on the Plexiglas™ they would dry flat, but there would then be no way to remove the print and mount from the Plexiglas™. The solution to this is to adhere a sheet of polyester cloth to the Plexiglas™, then the mount to the polyester cloth and finally the print to the mount. All these steps are done in immediate succession, and the last step is to protect the face of the print with waxed paper and roll the print flat with a roller. The whole "sandwich" is allowed to dry, the polyester cloth is then stripped from the Plexiglas™, and finally the polyester cloth is peeled away from the back of the mounted prints.

STEP 1: PREPARING THE STARCH PASTE

The adhesive used in this method is a paste made from boiled refined wheat starch. Wheat starch paste provides good adhesive properties, is easy to work with and is inexpensive. It is necessary to prepare the starch paste at least one day before it will be used. One brand of wheat starch that has been successfully used is Aytex P™, a powdered edible wheat starch manufactured by General Mills Chemicals, Inc. To prepare the paste, place 200 ml of wheat starch (volume measurement is convenient and sufficiently accurate) in a 4-quart enamel or glass saucepan. It is important that no iron or steel make contact with the starch solution at any stage in its preparation or use. Slowly and with constant stirring pour in 1400 ml of distilled or deionized water. Stir until there are no lumps and allow this mixture to sit overnight. An old wooden spoon that has been deacidified with magnesium bicarbonate is the best implement with which to stir starch pastes, both when cold and during cooking.

The following day, place the pan over a medium-low flame and stir until the mixture starts to thicken. The starch must be stirred constantly during its entire cooking phase or it will burn. After the mixture starts to thicken, cook with constant stirring over a low flame for 20 additional minutes. The properties of the gel that will form as well as the adhesive properties of starch pastes are determined by the length and the method of cooking, so it is important to follow the directions closely. After the mixture has cooked, add 0.4 ml of a saturated solution of thymol in methyl alcohol. Thymol is a fungicide and does not appear to affect the adhesive properties of the paste. Place the paste in a covered container and refrigerate. The paste may be used when cool and gelled, or may be refrigerated for up to one week before use.

To use the paste, the refrigerated gel must be diluted in a blender. Place the cold gel together with ⅔ of its volume of cold distilled water and blend for a few seconds at low speed, and then for 30-40 additional seconds at high speed. The paste thus formed is ready to use, and it should be kept covered to prevent a "skin" from forming and to keep out dust. It is most unpleasant to mount a print and discover particles of dirt or hardened starch trapped under the print. The prepared paste should be used on the same day.

THE ALBUMEN & SALTED PAPER BOOK

STEP 2: PREPARING THE RIGID PLEXIGLAS™ SUPPORT

The rigid support required for the purpose is a piece of ⁵⁄₁₆ or ⅜ inch Plexiglas™ somewhat larger than the total area of prints to be mounted. The Plexiglas™ is first prepared by sanding one surface with a waterproof sandpaper (200 grit) used wet, until it has assumed a matte surface. This roughened surface is necessary to allow the polyester cloth support to grip the plastic. To mount a print, first clean off the Plexiglas™ sheet with water and thoroughly dry it. Then apply an even coating of starch paste to the matte surface of the Plexiglas™. Do not use a brush that has an iron or steel band to hold the bristles; a flat Japanese brush or a foam brush should be used to apply the paste.

STEP 3: APPLYING THE POLYESTER CLOTH SUPPORT

The temporary cloth support used in this procedure is a single thickness of white polyester crepe, available in most fabric stores. This material is tightly woven and has a slight surface texture. It is used in sewing as a liner for garments. It must be larger than the piece of Plexiglas™ and it is helpful to make a seam around its perimeter to keep the cloth from unravelling. The polyester cloth must be laundered before each use.

Lay the cloth on the prepared Plexiglas™ by holding it by two opposite corners and bowing it in the center; let the middle touch down first and lower the corners until it lies flat on the Plexiglas™. Stretch it first in one direction and then the other. After working out the air bubbles as much as possible, apply an even layer of starch paste on top of the polyester. Take care that the cloth is now smooth, flat and free of bubbles.

STEP 4: APPLYING THE MOUNTING SHEET

The mount for albumen prints should be a sheet of heavy, smooth, all-rag paper of very high quality. The mount must first be pre-swelled by dampening it with a spray of distilled water, first on the front (watermark right-reading) side and then on the back side. The paper should get fairly wet and then be blotted between acid-free blotters. Pre-swelling helps to distribute the internal forces more evenly during drying. Note the grain direction of the mounting paper; the idea is to have the grain directions of the print and the mount crosswise to each other so that the tendency to curl is minimized and the print lies flatter. The grain direction of the unmounted print is always the direction of the print's natural curl.

To lay the pre-swelled mounting sheet on the polyester, grasp it by two opposite corners and place the center of the sheet down first. Lay the corners down with a rolling motion to try to force out any air bubbles. Smooth out the paper and apply another coating of starch paste on top of it. Experience will show what amount of paste is enough, but do not skimp or the print will not adhere satisfactorily. The use of too much paste will be apparent when the print is smoothed out.

STEP 5: APPLYING THE PRINT
Prints should be wetted with a spray of distilled water before mounting them. Spray both sides and blot them between sheets of acid-free blotting paper so that they are only damp when actually placed down on the mount. Remember to place the grain direction of the print perpendicular to that of the mount. The starch paste may need to be renewed by a fresh brushing over just before mounting. Leave room on the mounting paper between prints for hinges to be cut out later. As many prints as practical may be mounted on each large sheet of mounting paper.

Place waxed paper over the face of the prints and smooth them out with a hard rubber roller. Hold the waxed paper in place and start smoothing from the center of each print toward the edges. Large prints may require several sheets of waxed paper; overlap the sheets of waxed paper to prevent starch from reaching the face of the prints. Avoid excessive pressure in rolling or the paste will be forced out and the prints will not adhere to the mount. Peel off the waxed paper and remove any paste from the face of the prints using a ball of damp cotton.

Allow the whole "unit" to dry for at least 12 hours, depending on humidity, or until there is no "damp" smell from the starch. It is much better to be over-cautious in estimating when the prints are dry than too hasty. The pieces of Plexiglas™ may be placed upright to dry.

STEP 6: REMOVING THE MOUNTED PRINTS
FROM THE TEMPORARY SUPPORTS
When completely dry, the first step in removing the prints is to pull away the polyester cloth from all four sides of the Plexiglas™, up to the point where the mounting sheet begins. The grasp the polyester with two hands and pull it away at a low angle from the Plexiglas™ in one smooth motion. It is better to grasp the polyester across the short dimension of the mounting sheet and pull it the "long way," because this avoids unnecessary stress for the mounted prints.

When the polyester has been pulled off the Plexiglas™, turn the cloth over and gently peel the cloth away from the back of the mounting paper. Hold on to the paper to support it while peeling away the polyester. When the mounting sheet has been removed from the cloth, trim the mount to within 1/8 inch of the prints, allowing at the same time for two hinges 1 inch wide and 2 inches long on each print. The prints are now smooth, flat and ready for matting.

A CAUTIONARY NOTE:

Kolody's mounting method exerts considerable stress on the albumen layer of the print as it dries. While such stress does not usually harm prints, especially newly made prints, some 19th century prints may have a visibly weakened or severely cracked albumen layer. In this event mounting by Kolody's method is not recommended, because the stress of mounting may worsen the cracking of the albumen layer.

Print Storage

Prints are best stored in boxes and containers made especially for the purpose and sold by various suppliers to museums and libraries. Metal boxes are a good choice because they eliminate the danger of contamination from poor quality cardboard and wood itself. Metal boxes made for print storage are likely to be costly because special precautions are necessary in selecting and applying the finish on all metal surfaces. Storage boxes made from acid-free board are considerably less expensive, but may not have the durability required for use in a working collection. Vinyl covered print "cases" with metal clasps and hinges are more suitable to hard use, but may have to be re-lined with acid-free paper to insure a safe environment for prints. All prints should be sleeved or matted to protect them in storage.

Always be sure that no gases are emitted from paints or varnishes used on storage containers. Do not store prints in wooden cabinets on a long-term basis unless the cabinets are specially treated or metal-lined. Wooden cabinets may be thought of as large envelopes of the coarsest kind of paper. Gases that attack the paper support and the images of prints may also be present in the general environment of the room where prints are stored, and this must be taken into consideration in selecting the location of a print collection within a building. High levels of automobile exhaust[9] or ozone emitted from an electrostatic copier are both very destructive.

Anything that accompanies the prints in storage, especially inside the sleeves, should be of the highest quality. Do not store prints in the company of acidic or poor-quality papers or board, or together with adhesives, nitrate-base negatives or anything else likely to pollute the storage environment.

TEMPERATURE AND HUMIDITY CONTROL

The single most important consideration in print storage is that temperature and humidity should not undergo sudden drastic changes, and excessive heat and humidity should definitely be avoided. A satisfactory temperature and humidity range is 18-20°C at 35-45% RH. The reason why control of temperature and humidity is so important is the fact that these factors govern the *rate* of all possible destructive reactions that prints might undergo. The higher the temperature and humidity, the faster all the various mechanisms of deterioration will operate. Active control of temperature and humidity conditions is expensive, but is it the best and most necessary investment that any photographic collection can make.

CHAPTER 11

THE QUESTION OF PERMANENCE

THE LAST PRINT IN SILVER

'Tis the last print in Silver
Left mould'ring alone,
All her gold-toned companions
Are faded and gone.
No print of her kindred,
Albumen, is nigh,
To reflect back her jaundice
So sad to the eye.

I will leave thee, thou lone one,
To vanish away
And to all fellow-workers
With confidence say
Go, print now in Carbon,
Or platinum choose
As long recommended
By friend Jabez Hughes.

So soon may all follow
A 'Permanent way,'
And from out of our albums
No prints fade away.
For when Albumen's yellow,
and Chloride is flown,
Platino and Carbon
Shall still hold their own.

—Edgar Clifton, 1887[1]

The question of the durability of albumen and salted paper prints is of great interest to collectors, curators, librarians and historians, as well as to modern workers of these processes. This chapter deals with the historical record regarding the permanence of albumen and salted papers, and reviews the theoretical and practical considerations in guaranteeing maximum print stability

---

Historical Review

THE ERA OF SALTED PAPERS 1840-1855

During the late 1840's the initial burst of enthusiasm and interest of the general public for the new marvel—photographic pictures— had hardly worn off before the fading and staining of paper prints threatened to discredit photography on paper altogether, and reduce it to the status of a scientific curiosity. While daguerreotypes seemed to be fairly stable, the image on salted paper prints in many cases faded to near invisibility, and all sorts of complaints of staining and mottling were heard. It soon became apparent that something in the preparation and/or storage of a high percentage of photographic prints was leading to their speedy destruction. For various reasons the daguerreotype process was the most widely used for portraiture, but some commercial portraiture was attempted using Talbot's calotype process. The high prices paid for this service made the rapid fading of the results especially annoying to the patrons,[2] and the ensuing public complaints—together with Talbot's patent restrictions— effectively ended the commercial possibilities of calotype portraiture.

The real advantage of Talbot's negative-positive system of photography over the daguerreotype was the capability to make multiple copies of the image. Talbot himself took advantage of this in bringing out the first commercially offered photographically illustrated book, *The Pencil of Nature*, issued serially during the years 1844-1846. This was the first of several publications illustrated with salted paper prints that Talbot produced at his "Reading Establishment," where he had hired Nikolaas Henneman and Thomas Malone to carry out the actual printing. The prints made at Reading became some of the most visible and notorious examples of the instability of salted paper prints. A great many of the problems of the Reading prints may have stemmed from insufficient washing; Henneman himself stated in a discussion at a meeting of the Photographic Society of London in

May, 1856, that:

> We all know the "Pencil of Nature" alluded to by Mr. Malone; of those prints
> I made twenty-five in one batch; they had only three washings. Some of them
> remained perfectly good, as if they were printed but yesterday, and others
> have totally failed.[3]

Today of the surviving prints made for *The Pencil of Nature*, barely a handful are not very badly faded, and apparently none survive
in original condition. Many salted paper prints made by amateurs
at approximately the same period have survived much better than
The Pencil of Nature prints, pointing up the frequent occurrence that
mass-produced images get poorer fixing and washing than individual efforts.

Mostly for reasons of ease of operation and public preference, but
partly also because of the worry over fading, the daguerreotype retained complete dominance of commercial portraiture through the
early 1850's. Meanwhile, photographers struggled to improve both
the paper negative (which had already proved more adaptable to
outdoor photography than the daguerreotype) and the paper print.
Concern over print stability grew to become the single most press-
ing problem in photography, especially after advances in negative
technique in the late 1840's and early 1850's made the whole negative-
positive approach to photography so much more attractive.

Although progress had been made in determining the causes
of print fading, it was still very uncertain whether any given print
would survive for more than a few years. Determination of the exact
causes of fading was complicated by the vast number of different
base papers, binder materials and processing chemicals in use at that
time. One fact, however, was very clear; photographic paper negatives—in which the image was produced by development—had a
much better record of durability than the various kinds of printing-
out papers used for positives.[4] Nevertheless, the image color, famil-
iarity, superior tone reproduction and controllability of printing-out
papers insured their continued use while the search for improved
print stability went on.

In 1855 the Photographic Society of London established a committee to investigate the causes of print fading. The committee asked
for samples of prints made by any and all processes to be forwarded
to them for examination and testing. In its report the committee
stated:

Hence it appears that the most ordinary cause of fading, may be traced to the presence of sulphur, the source of which may be intrinsic from hyposulphite left in the print, or extrinsic from the atmosphere, and in either case the action is much more rapid in the presence of moisture.[5]

The "Committee Appointed to take into Consideration the Question of the Fading of Positive Photographic Pictures upon Paper" was first class, both in its eminent personnel and the accuracy of its conclusions. Its report spelled out for the photographic community several of the leading causes of print instability, and its practical recommendations laid stress on two important procedures: thorough washing of prints after fixing, and the employment of gold toning. Although these findings were hardly novel or completely original to the committee members, the authority the committee's work put behind these recommendations was very beneficial to the general practice of photography at that time.

During the same year—1855—another important key to print stability was discovered and published by two French photographers, Alphonse Davanne and Jules Girard. These two men contributed immeasurably to the advancement of photographic science by systematically examining all aspects of the printing process with the most up-to-date chemical and empirical methods of their time. They analyzed for sulfur content prints fixed in fresh sodium thiosulfate and others fixed in "old hypo," and confirmed the suspicions of many photographers that only fresh, pure thiosulfate solutions—followed by thorough washing—left prints uncontaminatedwith sulfur after processing. By subjecting test prints to high humidity levels they showed that the sulfur contaminated prints "rapidly turn yellow and at last vanish."[6]

THE INTRODUCTION OF ALBUMEN PAPER 1850-1860

Although the work of the printing committee of The Photographic Society of London and of Davanne and Girard (as well as other independent investigators) was successful in identifying the primary causes of fading, the problem of print instability did not end. In the mid 1850's a transition from salted papers to the new albumen paper took place, and albumen prints brought new difficulties in fixing and washing, mostly because of their thicker and less permeable image layer. The adoption of albumen paper meant that a new technology had to be learned, and naturally it required several years before the peculiarities of albumen paper became familiar to both photographers and the newly organized albumen paper manufacturing companies. The working methods for plain salted papers did not exactly coincide with those of albumen paper, especially in the sensitizing and toning steps. No doubt as a result of unfamiliarity with the material and the general uncertainty over proper fixing and washing procedures, a great many early albumen prints now exhibit advanced yellowing and fading.

The point which was most stressed in the journals of that period was the necessity of thorough washing, and it seems that probably most photographers took pains to wash their prints as best they could. It appears in retrospect that apart from the use of exhausted fixer solutions, the most serious detriments to permanence of prints during the decade of the 1850's were additives (mostly for their presumed toning effect) to the fixing bath. A large category of such additives were described as "coloring agents," but merely had the effect of decomposing the sodium thiosulfate, so that a process of sulfiding of the silver image took place.

Gold toning, which had the endorsement of the most respected photographic authorities and was certainly a good idea in principle, was often the fatal flaw in otherwise good processing because of the manner in which it was applied; when photographers mixed gold chloride and "hypo" together, in many cases the acidity of the gold solution decomposed the sodium thiosulfate and liberated sulfur, which ultimately caused the prints to fade (see Chapters 8 & 9). This method of toning was known as the *sel d'or* method, and it was the most widely used approach to gold toning in the decade 1850-1860. When the solutions were fresh and the work properly done, the combined toning and fixing of the *sel d'or* method occasionally produced prints of excellent stability, but in ordinary practice the method had too many drawbacks and was finally replaced at the end of the decade by the vastly superior "separate" toning approach.

The new technique of separate toning in alkaline gold chloride solutions—followed by fixation in fresh, strong sodium thiosulfate—was a great step forward that consolidated the advances in print stability made during the 1850's and allowed albumen paper to attain a much better record of resistance to fading than had been accomplished with the older plain salted papers. The new alkaline gold toners deposited more gold than the other toning methods, and this contributed to the resistance of albumen prints to oxidative fading. In addition to the protection offered by the gold, the albumen layer itself made a significant difference in protecting the silver image from oxidizing gases.

ALBUMEN PRINTS AFTER 1860

In the 1860's the old idea that the hypo bath was also a kind of "toning" bath finally gave way to the more modern view that its purpose was strictly to remove the light-sensitive substances remaining in the print. As the 1860's progressed the manufacture of albumen paper became more and more centralized in factories, and the overall quality of albumen paper increased as a result. Improvements in albumen coating procedures also resulted in glossier papers. Albumen prints from the 1860's were generally "salted" with 2-3% chloride, an amount considerably higher than was used later on in the 1880's and 1890's. This increased chloride content in the earlier prints on the whole resulted in slightly higher average print shadow densities, which in turn meant that relatively more silver was deposited to form the image. More image silver results in improved resistance to fading,[7] and albumen prints of the 1860's and 1870's seem to have accumulated a slightly better average record of durability (in terms of resistance to image fading) than their weakly salted and scantily exposed successors in the 1880's and 1890's. The reasons for the shift in chloride content of albumen paper have to do with changes in the character of the negatives used, and are discussed in Chapter 6.

ALBUMEN VERSUS EMULSION-TYPE PRINTING-OUT PAPERS

By the 1890's a feeling of mistrust for albumen paper was growing, since a significant number of prints from previous years were already yellowed or faded. The yellowing was particularly objectionable, because while fading could be ascribed to poor technique, yellowing seemed almost intrinsic to the material. When the new emulsion-type gelatin and collodion printing-out papers were introduced in the late 1880's, their makers trumpeted the "undoubted permanence" of these papers as loudly as their "convenience." As emulsion papers gained ground in the marketplace, scathing denunciations of albumen paper appeared in the photographic journals. "Judging from the abuse heaped upon the innocent albumen print by many writers for the journals, a stranger from the planet Mars would doubtless wonder why it is not immediately suppressed," wrote W. H. Sherman in the *American Annual of Photography* and *The Times Almanac* for 1892.[8] "According to these writers," he continued, "the head and front of its offending is its want of permanency.

The relative merits of each type of paper were hotly disputed and exaggerated claims were made on both sides. The debate recalled the furor which accompanied the introduction of the gelatin dry plate, and many of the arguments put forth in favor of albumen paper were similar to those used to defend the old wet collodion process, namely that photographers were used to albumen paper and could turn out albumen prints easier and cheaper than with the new emulsion papers. The difference in the case of the printing papers, however, was the issue of permanency; not only was albumen paper inconvenient because of the necessity to sensitize it before use, it also had the undeniable tendency to yellow in the highlight areas. For a while the low price of albumen paper kept its sales strong, but by 1895 cutthroat competition among producers lowered the price of the gelatin and collodion printing-out papers[9] and the outcome was clear: albumen paper began to be outsold by the emulsion papers and was on the road to obsolescence.

Ironically, at this time when the producers of gelatin and collodion emulsion-type printing-out papers were proclaiming the superior permanence of their product over albumen paper, they were also recommending combined toning-fixing baths, a circumstance that definitely did not maximize print stability. Many gelatin and collodion prints of this era are now in rather poor condition as a result of the "combined bath" (which long before had been repudiated for use with albumen paper), although after the mid 1890's many unfavorable reports on this technique discouraged professionals from using it. Apart from this difficulty, however, the gelatin and collodion printing-out papers lived up to their manufacturers' claims and have established an excellent record of stability, with collodion papers proving exceptionally stable. Although collodion printing-out papers have a thin emulsion layer composed of essentially the same material—cellulose nitrate—that has proven so impermanent and dangerous when used as a film base for sheet and motion picture films, there is absolutely no evidence to suggest that collodion paper prints are in any way dangerous or unstable.

Some of the defenders of albumen paper preferred it out of habit, while others argued that its long tonal scale and unique qualities of image color, surface, etc., were valuable in their own right, apart from considerations of cost and convenience. The modern reader is most apt to be sympathetic to this position, since today many people admire the "special" character of albumen printing paper in spite of yellowing of the highlights and the many instances of fading found in surviving prints. Many critics of albumen paper in the 1890's put forward the completely erroneous view that since such a large number of early albumen prints had faded, *all* albumen prints can expect the same fate sooner or later. The more well-informed of these speaking on behalf of albumen paper reminded the critics that back in the 1850's proper toning, fixing and washing procedures for albumen paper were not well understood.

Figure 46.
An 1899 advertisement for collodio-chloride emulsion type printing-out paper. The reference to "permanency" was directed at albumen paper users.

Highlight Yellowing in Albumen Prints

The most common form of deterioration of historical albumen prints is the appearance of a yellow or yellowish-brown stain in the highlights (non-image areas). While the severity of yellowing varies widely from print to print, it is probably safe to say that not a single albumen print survives from the 19th century without some degree of staining in non-image areas. Many prints, it is true, do seem to be pristine and unyellowed, but when compared side by side with a freshly albumenized (and never sensitized) sheet of paper, a noticeable difference will be perceived between the "paper white" areas in the freshly albumenized sheet and the historical print.

Most albumen prints do not require a comparison with a freshly albumenized sheet, because it is quite obvious that they have yellowed. Approximately 85% of extant albumen prints made after 1860 display what might be called "moderate to severe" yellowing, while the remaining 15% or so *seem* to have white highlights unless compared side by side with a white sheet of paper. For those albumen prints made in the 1850's the figures probably are closer to 95% and 5%. These figures are not based on any formal statistical sampling, merely on the accumulated experience of the author in examining prints and through discussions with curators and collectors. A statistical study of a large collection of albumen prints with regard to the type and severity of print deterioration—including highlight yellowing—would be a most welcome addition to the literature of photographic preservation.

Yellowing of the highlights in albumen prints is sometimes *independent* of generalized image fading, i.e. the highlights have turned yellow but the middletones and shadows have remained apparently unchanged. Highlight yellowing is so prevalent in albumen prints that it often serves as an important clue in their identification since the highlight yellowing phenomenon is peculiar to albumen paper and does not occur in quite the same way in otherwise similar gelatin and collodion papers.

Severe highlight yellowing is accompanied in most cases by an apparent color shift and density loss in the image itself. The original purplish brown color of many prints has lost density and faded to a sepia brown. Loss of highlight detail is also common in such cases. The image color may even assume a greenish tinge. Indeed few albumen prints today at all resemble their original image color.

The time period required for the onset of highlight yellowing in an albumen print appears to vary considerably, and is probably affected primarily by the moisture level and temperature of the storage environment and the amount of residual thiosulfate and silver-thiosulfate complexes present. Many prints seem to have yellowed very quickly—within one or two years of processing—while others seem to have taken much longer. There is no guarantee that even today improper storage will not initiate rapid yellowing in the prints that have remained reasonably unyellowed up to this point. Photographic literature of the period 1860-1895 does contain numerous mentions and complaints about the yellowing of highlights in albumen paper, although it seems clear that nowhere near 85% of prints had yellowed to a "moderate to severe" extent during the period when albumen paper was still in general use.

CAUSES OF HIGHLIGHT YELLOWING
IN ALBUMEN PRINTS

The probable origin of the yellowing phenomenon in albumen paper is the chemical bonding of silver to sulfur-containing side groups on the protein molecules of albumen, some of which have a very high affinity for silver. The silver bonded during sensitization to these sites on the protein is so tightly held that treatment in hypo is not sufficient to remove it. Thus a small amount of silver remains in all areas of a fixed albumen print; the conversion of this silver to silver sulfide is the immediate cause of the yellowing phenomenon.

The first published notice of the presence of residual silver in non-image areas of albumen prints was made in December 1859 by Davanne and Girard.[10] In a communication on the general subject of the fixation of positive prints to the French Photographic Society, the two scientists noted that a 2% solution of potassium cyanide did remove all traces of silver from albumen prints, while strong solutions of hypo did not. They wrote:

> These results present a certain importance; . . . they show that it is difficult to remove every trace of silver salt contained in albumenised proofs, and consequently, explain the difficulty which photographers often meet with in their attempts to obtain proofs on albumenised paper in which the whites shall be pure and well preserved.[11]

They also noted that cyanide fixation had two serious drawbacks which virtually ruled it out as a practical technique: it attacked and severely bleached the silver image, and it was highly poisonous.

In 1866 Matthew Carey Lea, the famous American photographic scientist, also noted the presence of residual silver in albumen prints. He conducted a series of experiments to find an appropriate solvent for this retained silver, but with no success.[12]

The question was explored by the Englishman John Spiller, who wrote in a paper, which he read to the Photographic Society of Great Britain on Jan. 14, 1868:

> My experiments went to prove that the metal was retained in the whites of the albumen print, and indeed in all parts of the coating, in the form of an argentic organic compound, colorless, unalterable by light, and comparatively insoluble in hyposulphites and other fixing agents. It could not be a simple sulphide, for the test by which I discovered its existence in the paper was the production of a brown stain upon moistening the white surface with sulphide of ammonium.[13]

Twenty-five years later two Englishmen, A. Haddon and F. B. Grundy, followed up on the inquiries made by Spiller by actually measuring the amount of silver retained in prints that were sensitized and fixed, but never exposed. These prints should have contained no silver at all, since they had no visible image. The results of their study were shocking, because they found that an unexposed print (that had been thoroughly fixed and washed) still contained nearly 5% of the silver left after sensitization and before processing.[14] To demonstrate the significance of this finding they took an unexposed and fixed sheet of albumen paper and first converted the residual silver to silver chloride by placing the print in chlorine water; they then applied a solution of potassium nitrite to act as a chlorine acceptor and proceeded to print out an image that was nearly as intense as one printed in the usual way! They reported these disturbing findings in a series of articles in the *British Journal of Photography* in the mid 1890's.[15]

If the assumption made by Spiller and confirmed by Haddon and Grundy is true, then the large amounts of "silver albumenate" present in all areas of albumen prints are very threatening to the longterm stability of these materials, since therefore the potential for very severe highlight staining exists in every print. The presumed mechanism of the yellowing is the formation of silver sulfide by reaction of the albumen-bound silver with labile sulfur supplied by residual fixer or atmospheric pollution. If a print was inadequately fixed or washed, then probably it will yellow in the highlights in addition to fading, and this kind of yellow staining can and does occur in gelatin and collodion as well as albumen prints.

Under such circumstances of high levels of residual fixer, albumen prints can be expected to display relatively more severe highlight yellowing than gelatin prints because of the extra silver available in the highlight areas to react with sulfur from the decomposing residual fixer. After 75 years (roughly the period of time that has elapsed since the last widespread use of glossy albumen paper) the highly fixer-contaminated albumen prints are no doubt already deteriorated and obviously little can be done of a preventative nature to preserve them. For these prints restoration by chemical means is the only hope, but this task is beyond our present abilities.

ASSESSING THE RATE OF YELLOWING AND FADING

At present we must concentrate on the prevention of further decay by striving to understand more completely the mechanisms of fading, yellowing and staining. As a first step it is important to assess whether the yellowing process is ongoing for all surviving albumen prints (as theoretically it would be, since some sulfur is present in the atmosphere of nearly every locality), and if so, at what rate. This cannot be done visually, and in fact it is a property of human vision that has probably kept the problem of highlight staining of albumen prints from receiving more attention than it has.

The human visual system has a built-in mechanism that automatically seeks out the lightest area in a photographic print and pegs that as a "reference white;" this adaptive mechanism can lead an observer to believe that the highlights of a print are brighter than they are unless a side-by-side comparison is made with a "true" white. It is indeed fortunate for our appreciation of albumen paper photographs that we have this built-in ability to compensate for stained highlights, since otherwise a majority of albumen photographs would seem excessively "flat" and lifeless.

On the other hand the imperceptibly slow fading process and staining of the highlights in historical albumen prints may be proceeding at a rate which will lead to very severe image deterioration long before the paper and albumen substrata deteriorate. What this means is that possibly in another 75 years, not a single albumen print will at all resemble its original appearance. Without a monitoring program no one has any idea how rapidly further deterioration will occur. Such a monitoring program might consist of checking a statistically significant sample of albumen prints in several collections by measuring reflection densities in image and non-image areas. The densitometers should be equipped with red, green, blue and visual equivalent filters, and the same prints should be rechecked at two, five, and ten year intervals.

Another benefit from a greater understanding of the causes of highlight yellowing and overall fading would be information about the best way to store albumen prints, i.e., what are the most beneficial types of filing enclosures, framing practices, etc., in order to minimize further fading and yellowing. The reversal of yellowing that has already occurred is an extremely difficult task, principally because the silver sulfide which forms the yellow stain is much more chemically stable than the colloidal silver of the image itself. No presently known treatment can remove the highlight yellowing without completely altering the character of the print.

Generalized Image Fading

The second most prevalent kind of deterioration—and the most serious for the informational and aesthetic value of the photograph—is generalized image fading. The principal internal causes for this condition in albumen prints are the same as in other photographic materials, namely residual thiosulfate and silver-thiosulfate complexes which have been allowed to remain in the material through inadequate fixing and washing. Moreover, albumen prints are also subject to fading induced by external causes, either

1) sulfiding of the image from atmospheric sulfur compounds such as sulfur dioxide, etc., and

2) oxidation fading caused by oxidizing gases such as ozone, organic solvents, etc. Albumen prints do not respond to the so-called "bleach and redevelopment" methods which have been successful in restoring sulfided gelatin-based develop-out photographic materials. The problems with the "bleach and redevelopment" method in regard to albumen prints are that the residual silver in the highlight areas redevelops along with the image, the "redevelopment" step does not provide sufficient density overall, and finally, the color of the "restored" image is black and therefore totally out of character with the original color of the print.

Deterioration Caused by Defective Mounts and Mounting Adhesives

A third major type of deterioration afflicting albumen prints originates from poor quality mounting boards and improper mounting adhesives. These problems are serious ones because approximately 95% of all albumen prints were mounted at the time of their production. Many mounting boards used in the 19th century were composed of thin top and bottom layers of relatively good quality paper laminated to a thick core of pulp containing a high percentage of lignin. The decomposition products of lignin migrate through the top layer of the board and attack the photograph, causing staining and brittleness and accelerating and fading and yellowing of the silver image. In many cases the use of putrified starch or gelatin adhesives accomplished the same kinds of deterioration.

Other problems associated with mounts are reddish stains known as "foxing" and stains caused by mold or fungus growth. At the moment the repertoire of preservation treatments available to photographic conservators for use with albumen prints is somewhat limited; the removal of prints from obviously defective mounts and their careful remounting onto appropriate mounts with safe adhesives is the only technique for the preservation of albumen prints that has proven itself in practice. Remounting, however, does nothing to reverse the deterioration that has already occurred.

The Need for Restoration Research

The reversal of yellowing, fading and staining caused by all of the above internal and external factors continues to be beyond the present state of knowledge in the field of photographic conservation. In spite of the enormous cultural importance of the photographic record of the 19th century and the advanced state of deterioration in which many albumen prints exist today, no research into the nature of the problems or the potential for new restoration techniques has been done since the days of Haddon and Grundy.

The reasons for this lack of research may be traced to the obsolescence of albumen paper by 1900 and the attitudes which prevailed for most of the 20th century toward photographic preservation. Within 10 years of the work done by Haddon and Grundy two revolutionary changes took place in the technology of photographic printing papers. Albumen paper was replaced by somewhat similar gelatin and collodion printing-out papers in the mid 1890's, and these in turn were supplanted by gelatin developing-out papers (of the type still in use) by 1905. Naturally scientific attention turned to these materials, and the problems of albumen were forgotten. Much research has been done concerning the permanence of gelatin-based printing papers, but there is no certainty of the applicability of these results to albumen-based materials. Although the chemical and physical characteristics of albumen prints are similar in some ways to gelatin prints, there are a number of significant differences. It is now apparent that at least the restoration techniques used on gelatin prints are inappropriate for albumen prints.

The lack of organized research into the problems of albumen prints may also be explained by previously held attitudes toward the importance of 19th-century photographs. For many years the deterioration of these artifacts was ignored, and photographic copies of important images were considered by many to be a completely satisfactory substitute for the original photograph. The several new factors which in recent years have begun to change these attitudes—a new appreciation of the aesthetic dimension of 19th-century photography, a new emphasis on preservation of original photographic artifacts, and the greatly progressed decay which has beset surviving prints—now make it more imperative that some inquiries into the specific problems of albumen prints be conducted. The reward of success in such research would be that the wonderful beauty of albumen prints could be preserved for generations to come, instead of comprising an unfortunate footnote to the history of photography.

AFTERWORD TO THE 2ᴺᴰ EDITION

———•———

It has now been 32 years since the first edition of the *Albumen and Salted Paper Book* appeared in 1980. This second edition has no significant changes from the first, except for the change in publisher—now the RIT Cary Graphic Arts Press—and this brief author's afterword. During the intervening years, I have spent my entire career at Rochester Institute of Technology pursuing research into the preservation of photographs, recorded information of other types, and of cultural property in general. It has been my privilege to be the founding director of RIT's Image Permanence Institute and a professor in the College of Imaging Arts and Sciences at RIT. My second book on 19th-century photography, *Care and Identification of 19th-Century Photographic Prints*, was published in 1986 by the Eastman Kodak Company.

It has also been my good fortune to receive grants from the National Endowment for the Humanities, the Smithsonian Institute of Museum and Library Services, and the Andrew W. Mellon Foundation to study the mechanisms of deterioration and methods for preservation of albumen prints and other forms of photographic images. I have learned much more about the deterioration and preservation of albumen and salted paper prints and, together with my colleagues and collaborators, published much on the subject.

When the opportunity arose to create a second edition of the *Albumen and Salted Paper Book*, my first reaction was that the changes needed to bring the book into accordance with what I had learned in 30 years would be extensive. Ultimately, I came to realize that the book stands up very well in its original form. The only new material I felt to be necessary was some reflection and perspective on the aspects of it that deal with preservation; therefore I have added this author's afterword to the second edition. The book's original preface has been retained, so this is the place to acknowledge those who helped bring the second edition into print: David Pankow, Director of the RIT Cary Graphic Arts Press, Molly Cort, Managing Editor, Lisa Mauro, Designer. Lauren Parish of the Image Permanence Institute at RIT provided invaluable help in proofing and correcting this second edtion. I thank them for their vision and efforts to make this edition a reality.

As the preface to the first edition states, the book is both a how-to and a technical history. The recipes for making albumen and salted paper prints were refined through my own experience, and they work. During the last three decades, the public's interest in "old processes" has waxed and waned, but has never gone away. I think the present time is a period of greater interest than ever before, partly because more young people have come of age without the opportunity to make images of any kind by chemical means. The combination of hand-craft and technology required in making a salted paper or albumen print is alluring and thrilling, and will remain so regardless of the latest innovations in digital imaging.

Concerning the history of printing technology during the period 1840 – 1895, I also feel that it does not require revision in this second edition. The sources I read and cited in the book remain a very good starting point for any future scholars who may wish to revisit the subject. I might seek other sources or re-read them now with slightly different eyes, or a more nuanced understanding, but I believe the book as written presents both the technical history and the how-to information as a record or document of the process of learning and darkroom practice I went through in the late 1970's. In that sense, the book is a kind of journal of my voyage of discovery, one that should not be altered to add a little bit here or correct a minor misunderstanding there.

The first edition book went beyond the historical and the how-to and talked about subjects relating to preservation of prints and the legacy that 19th-century photography left for future generations. It is in these areas—mainly discussed in Chapters 10 and 11—where I

THE ALBUMEN & SALTED PAPER BOOK

would add some thoughts and corrections and where my subsequent experience shows that the information was on less solid ground than the recipes and the historical literature references. I still feel the book as originally published should be reprinted in its entirety. I hope the thoughts added in this afterword will address some misapprehensions and also provide the reader with another interesting contrast—the passage of 30 years. In truth, the majority of what was written in Chapters 10 and 11 is still valuable and correct as I understand those subjects today. (It was a little shocking to realize that I hadn't learned all that much in 30 years).

Chapter 10 deals with finishing, mounting and storage. Nothing needs to be said about the historical sections of this chapter. However, the latter sections beginning with "A Contemporary Approach to Finishing, Display, and Storage" and continuing to the end of the chapter, do merit some comment. Polyester sleeves and 100% rag mat board are still appropriate choices for print enclosures. But hinging with Japanese tissue, although still in use by conservators, is but one of many approaches and it is best left to a professional to decide when its use is warranted. The following section, "A Conservator's Mounting Method" is likewise not to be taken as a safe or routine procedure that is recommended for albumen or other prints by people without advanced training or experience. There has been an enormous development of knowledge about the conservation of photographs during the last 30 years. We have learned more about the tendency of albumen layers to crack, a factor which complicates mounting procedures. One may experiment with one's own self-created prints, but the major lesson I would now impart to the reader—especially with actual historical objects—is to leave anything so invasive as the Plexiglas™ starch mounting of a print to a seasoned professional. David Kolody's mounting method in Chapter 10 was in keeping with the profession's knowledge and practice of the time (late 1970's) but the reader would do well to investigate the subject much more thoroughly than I did at that time. The American Institute for Conservation of Art and Historic Artifacts in Washington, D.C. maintains a website with guidance on how contact a professional conservator.

The sections on print storage and proper environments in Chapter 10 were brief and did not contain any major statements that I later learned to be untrue. In these few paragraphs, though, were the seeds of much of my subsequent career. The message that the best care of prints arises from a combination of inert, but functional enclosures and appropriate temperature and humidity conditions was and is true. All the experiments later performed on albumen and salted paper prints at the Image Permanence Institute bore out the importance of these concepts.

To the reader of this second edition, I would only point to some subtle but important refinements. Proper enclosures do not, in themselves, guarantee survival of prints in good condition. Enclosures can mitigate light, handling damage, atmospheric contaminants and dust, but a humid and warm environment can undo all the expense and effort of other preservation measures. The recommended relative humidity range in Chapter 10 of 35-45% is still very sound advice. We know now that albumen and salted paper prints—indeed all silver prints of any kind—are vulnerable to silver oxidation at RHs much above 55% or so. We also have come to realize that oxidation (a form of metal corrosion) is the most common cause of print fading by far. Therefore, the humidity of the storage environment is the most important single factor in preserving 19th-century silver prints, though effective preservation also involves utilizing a combination of good enclosures and handling practices.

Regarding temperature, it was correctly stated in Chapter 10 that temperature and relative humidity govern the *rate* of all possible chemical reactions of deterioration, including silver oxidation. Chapter 10 recommends near room temperature (68-72°F, 18-20°C) as a satisfactory condition for storage. That is true, but cooler conditions are even better, providing that the humidity can be controlled to the proper range mentioned above. The statements made about environmental conditions in Chapter 10 are concepts that have resonated and proven true over the decades.

In Chapter 11, "The Question of Permanence," the historical review of the issue once again points the reader to important and reasonable comprehensive original sources. They are what they are, and do reflect the state of knowledge at the time of their writing. That is also the case with my own statements about the causes of fading and staining of albumen and salted paper prints in this book. At that time, I was a practitioner who had made a close reading of the 19th-century literature. My views could not help but be influenced by what I read and even by what I had been taught by the teachers I studied with to learn the contemporary practices of black and white photography.

But I later did go on to make a close study of the causes of fading and staining in albumen prints, as well as many other kinds of silver images on film, paper, and resin-coated paper supports. Chapter 11 deals at some length with the phenomenon of yellowing in the white area of albumen prints. This yellowing behavior is, as the chapter explains, unique to albumen prints in that it is nearly universally found in surviving prints today. Prints with gelatin or collodion binders (emulsions) can, and often do, develop yellowish stains. In these instances, the staining is visually related to either the presence of residual thiosulfate or silver thiosulfate (from exhausted fixing baths, or to the oxidation and migration of silver). All types of silver prints are potentially subject to highlight yellowing and staining from this cause. Chapter 11 points to this as the major cause of albumen prints yellowing, which it is not. The principal (and unique to albumen) cause is due to reactions between the egg white proteins and sugars also present in egg white. This is the so-called "Maillard Reaction". Not all albumen prints have yellowed to the same degree. Some are still quite white in the highlights. I think Chapter 11 rather overstates when it says "possibly in another 75 years, not a single albumen print will at all resemble its original appearance." Thirty of those 75 years have already passed without evidence of the correctness of that speculation.

In Chapter 11, the issue of albumen yellowing is ascribed mainly to fixing and washing problems (insufficient rinsing in water and the use of exhausted fixer and/or gold toning baths that included thiosulfate). These topics were discussed at great length in the 19th-century literature. Determining the amount of residual silver or residual thiosulfate in albumen prints was an extremely challenging problem for 19th-century chemical analysis. Debates about the role of silver-albumen compounds and residual silver were hot topics during the 1890's. Since my own knowledge came mostly from reading the historical literature, I repeated those ideas in Chapter11. My current understanding on albumen yellowing is this: albumen prints, like all silver prints, can become stained and yellowed from insufficient washing and use of exhausted fixer solutions. However, insufficient washing is less common with albumen prints than later silver papers because albumen prints have a quite thin paper support. The difficult thing in washing fixer out of prints is to remove it from the paper support, which soaks up the fixer substance and releases it into the wash water much more slowly than the very thin albumen layer does. Careless overuse of fixing baths past the point of exhaustion also occurred with albumen prints but all mid-19th-century literature warns very strongly against it.

Because of the protein-sugar reaction all albumen layers tend to yellow. They do not yellow to the same degree because of two factors. Chapter 11 correctly states that environmental conditions affect the rate and extent of yellowing. The second factor is that the residual sugar in albumen probably varied from print to print because albumen was often fermented prior to coating, during which natural yeasts consumed some amount of sugar (see Chapter 4). So, it is the nature of albumen prints to yellow but other aspects of photographic processing and silver image deterioration can also play a role.

Perhaps the biggest area where Chapter 11 omits or at least greatly misleads by understatement, is the fundamental question of why and how albumen and salted paper prints fade. What is meant by "fading" is unwelcome change in the silver image itself. This may take the form of simply getting lighter overall until details of the image simply disappear. It also usually means changes in color, especially toward a more brownish or yellowish hue. Chapter 11 correctly states that nearly all surviving albumen prints are faded to one degree or another. Despite the extensive discussion of fixing and washing in the 19th-century (and later) literature, research has clearly shown that silver image oxidation is the principal reason why so many albumen prints—and other types of silver images as well—are faded. Oxidation of silver is a greater threat to silver printing-out papers because of the relatively small size of the silver image particles when compared to developed-out images. This is especially true for the highlight areas of the image. In the lighter tones of printing-out papers there is less silver present overall than in darker areas and it can be more easily corroded by moisture in combination with atmospheric contaminants. Of course, poor processing can also be a factor but is not the principal cause of fading. The importance of oxidation as a mechanism of deterioration in silver images became very well understood in the 1980's. The use of transmission electron microscopy to study particle size and shape, together with accelerated aging using heat, humidity and oxidizing atmospheres also greatly clarified the behavior of albumen prints. Thanks to that research, we now place much greater emphasis on avoiding oxidation through proper storage environments and more hope that we can preserve the great legacy of 19th-century photography for generations to come. Some of the published research that is involved with this process is listed on the following page.

James M. Reilly
October 2012

References dealing with the stability of albumen prints and silver images published since the completion of this book:

Reilly, J.M., Nishimura, D.W., Adelstein, P.Z., and Cupriks, K., "The Stability of Black-and-White Photographic Images, with Special Reference to Microfilm," Abbey Newsletter, Vol.12, No.5, (July 1988).

Reilly, J., Kennedy, N., Black, D, and Van Dam, T., "Image Structure and Deterioration in Albumen Prints," *Photographic Science and Engineering*, Vol. 28 (4), (1984), pp. 166-171.

Reilly, J., "Role of the Maillard, or 'Protein-Sugar' Reaction in Highlight Yellowing of Albumen Photographic Prints," Preprints of the 10th Annual Meeting of the AIC, Milwaukee, WI. (1982), pp. 160-168.

Reilly, J., "Albumen Prints: A Summary of New Research About Their Preservation," Picturescope, Vol. 30, (1982) pp.34-36.

Reilly, J., "The Albumen Print," Camera (Luzern), (Feb. 1979). Accompanied by six original photographs on albumen paper by the author.

Reilly, J., "The Manufacture and Use of Albumen Paper," *Journal of Photographic Science*, Vol. 6, (1977) pp. 156-151.

APPENDIX A

"It does one good to think how photographers, even while exercising the new art for money, have pursued it with a generous ardor for its own sake, and emulate each other in the magnanimity with which they throw their own discoveries into the common heap, and scorn to check the progress of their art for any selfish motive."

—Henry Morley and W.H. Wills, 1853[1]

———————

Fortunately the processes described in this book belonged to an era of individual experimentation with photographic materials, and the results of these individual efforts were often reported openly in books and journals of the day. Of course, many individuals and companies did choose to retain secrets about the exact methods they used, but it is quite possible to obtain a good general picture of historical technical practice by reading original books, pamphlets, letters and journals. The following are some suggestions for further reading, together with some brief notes about the kind of information available from each source.

———————

Surveys of the Technical History of Printing-Out Papers

Fritz Wentzel, *Memoirs of a Photochemist*, American Museum of Photography, Philadelphia (1960). This wonderful book is perhaps the most complete and satisfactory introduction in the English language to the technical history of photographic materials. The chapters on printing-out papers are well written and extensively annotated. They are condensed from the author's own experiences as a production supervisor in many different photographic paper factories (beginning in 1914, when albumen paper was still being manufactured), and from his research for the work he co-authored with J.M. Eder, *Die photographischen Kopirverfabren mit Silbersalzen (Positiv-Prozess)*, 1928 edition (see below).

Josef Maria Eder, *The History of Photography*, Columbia University Press, N. Y. (1945), trans. by Edward Epstean. Chapter 74 (pp. 534-539) of this monumental work deals with the history of printing-out processes with silver salts. This is an excellent place to begin a program of further study because it gives the landmark steps in the development of these processes and also provides the references where the first notice of these processes was published.

Josef Maria Eder and Fritz Wentzel, *Die photographischen Kopirverfahren mit Silbersalzen (Positiv-Prozess)*, Wilhelm Knapp, Halle (1928). This book, which is also known as Book IV, Part I of the 3rd edition of J.M. Eder's multivolume *Ausführliches Handbuch der Photographie* is the most complete technical and historical account of silver printing-out processes ever written. Unfortunately, it has never been translated into English. It and the references cited in it are the source of a great deal of the material in *The Albumen and Salted Paper Book*. Editions previous to the 1928 edition were authored by Eder alone, but thanks to the efforts of Dr. Fritz Wentzel, the 1928 edition is the largest and most complete.

———————•———————

Early Writings About Salted Papers

Robert Hunt, *A Manual of Photography*, Richard Griffin & Co., Glasgow (1854), 4th edition. The many editions of Hunt's *Manual of Photography* offer a comprehensive glimpse of the state of photographic manipulation at these early dates, and include a great many recipes for different kinds of printing papers. This is a good work in which to see the *diversity* of photographic experimentation at this time.

Thomas Sutton, *The Calotype Process, A Hand Book to Photography on Paper,* Joseph Cundall, London (1855). Sutton's calotype manual was another often reprinted and updated work that—unlike Hunt's far-ranging *Manual*—concentrates on what appear to be the most tried and true methods of the day for paper negatives and positives. This book kept its popularity through at least 10 editions and seems fairly representative of general practice. The 1855 edition also contains directions for albumenizing paper.

W.H. Thornthwaite, *A Guide to Photography,* Home & Thornthwaite, London (1856), 10th ed. Thornthwaite's *Guides* were also extremely popular and influential during the early 1850's. Either this work or Sutton's *The Calotype Process* will provide a good introduction to the printing techniques of the period.

The Albumen Print

Henry Peach Robinson and William DeWiveleslie Abney, *The Art and Practice of Silver Printing,* E. & H. T. Anthony, N. Y. (1881). This fine book is one of the best general texts On albumen and salted paper printing written in the 19th century. It is also very accessible to modern readers because it is part of the Arno Press reprint series of historical photographic books.

John Towler, *The Silver Sunbeam,* Joseph H. Ladd, N. Y. (1864). Towler's *Silver Sunbeam* is available in a reprint edition from Morgan & Morgan (1969) and contains a good general account of albumen and salted paper printing. Although it does not give as detailed a treatment of printing processes as Robinson and Abney's book does, it conveys a representative technical account of albumen printing in the Civil War era. It proved to be a very influential book in its own time.

Hermann W. Vogel, *Handbook of the Practice and Art of Photography,* Benerman & Wilson, Philadelphia (1875), 2nd edition. Vogel's *Handbook* was an English translation of a German original that was one of the best and most influential books on photographic technique written in the 19th century. It was as influential all over the world during the 1870's as Towler's *Silver Sunbeam* had been in America during the 1860's. Like many manuals of the era it does not contain a great deal about the methods used to *prepare* albumen paper, but there is much in it on the use of albumen paper. This reflects the shift to factory-coated albumen paper which was virtually complete by the year 1870.

Matthew Carey Lea, *A Manual of Photography,* privately printed for the author, Philadelphia (1871), 2nd edition. M. Carey Lea's *Manual* was the American equivalent to Vogel's *Handbook.* In fact, the two men were similarly regarded as among the most brilliant and learned men on photography in their respective countries. Both had reputations as eminent scientists and made basic discoveries that advanced the progress of photography. The general manuals that each wrote are also similar in scope and content (although in later years Vogel's *Handbook* expanded into 2 volumes in the German editions), and a comparison of the two is instructive regarding the approaches to photography in the United States and Germany in the 1870's.

Charles W. Hearn, *The Practical Printer,* Benerman & Wilson, Philadelphia (1874). Most of the other books on albumen printing in this list were written *for* professional photographers; this is one written *by* a professional photographer, who worked his way up from a studio apprentice to become a national authority on silver printing. The book is a very comprehensive treatment of the operations of printing with albumen and salted papers as it was actually done in American galleries of the 1870's. In addition to the usual recipes, etc., Hearn's own experiences are anecdotally recounted through the book, and his writing has a unique, down-to-earth style.

———•———

Matte Salted Papers

Arthur Freiherr von Hübl, *Der Silberdruck auf Salzpapier,* Wilhelm Knapp, Halle (1896). There is probably no more comprehensive and useful book about matte salted papers than Hübl's classic, *Der Silberdruck auf Salzpapier* (Silver Printing with Salted Papers). This was one of the most influential technical books published in connection with the revival of salted papers that took place at the end of the 19th century. Although no English translation was ever published, Hübl's style is simple and direct enough that a determined non-German speaking reader (armed with a German dictionary and perhaps a smattering of the German language) can obtain a great deal of useful information from the book. The book is divided into two parts, a theoretical section and a collection of recipes, and both parts are first rate in their scope and utility.

Lyonel Clark, *Platinum Toning*, Hazell, Watson & Viney, London (1890). Lyonel Clark was a very important figure in the revival of matte salted papers in the 1890's, and he contributed greatly to their popularity by pioneering the use of platinum toning for silver printing-out papers. The brown and black tones resulting from the use of platinum toners harmonized well with the other qualities of matte salted papers. Much more comprehensive than the title indicates, Clark's book was well received and functioned as the technical and aesthetic guidebook for the salted paper revival in the English-speaking world. *Platinum Toning* is sprinkled with the acerbic observations of the photographic scene for which Clark was well known. One example:

> Photographic amateurs are, I regret to say, an extremely lazy lot, with an increasing and morbid desire to produce quantity—an appetite largely encouraged by the pack of traders and process-mongers who live on their prey's credulity. (pp. 38-39)

APPENDIX B

Equipment

Centigram balance
50 ml buret
Glassware
Laboratory magnetic stirrer (optional)

Chemicals

Distilled water
Silver Nitrate, $AgNO_3$, 0.1 Normal
Sodium thiocyanate, NaCNS, or Potassium thiocyanate,
KCNS, 0.2 Normal
Ferric ammonium sulfate, saturated solution
Nitric acid, 6 Molar

Process

IMPORTANT SAFETY PRECAUTION:
Always wear approved laboratory eye protection and work in a
well ventilated area.

STEP 1: STANDARDIZATION OF THE THIOCYANATE
SOLUTION
1. Mix approximately 0.2 Normal sodium thiocyanate (16.2 g/liter) or potassium thiocyanate (19.4 g/liter) using distilled water. Note: Since both these chemicals are extremely hygroscopic, do not rely on the dry weight to give solutions of the correct normality. An analytical balance is not required to weigh out these amounts; a centigram balance should be sufficient.

2. Closely estimate the exact normality of the thiocyanate solution by titrating it into a silver nitrate solution of known normality:

> **a.** Put 35 ml of 0.1 Normal silver nitrate solution into a small flask. To make a 0.1 Normal silver nitrate solution, add 4.25 g silver nitrate to enough distilled water to make a total volume of 250 ml.
>
> **b.** Add 1 ml of saturated ferric ammonium sulfate solution.
>
> **c.** Add 5 ml of 6 Molar nitric acid. Note: To make 6 Molar nitric acid, add 100 ml of concentrated nitric acid (15.78N) to 163 ml of water.
>
> **d.** Run in thiocyanate from a buret until a faint brownish color appears and will not disappear with vigorous stirring. Note the volume of thiocyanate at this point.
>
> **e.** Calculate the normality of the thiocyanate using the following equation:

milliequivalents of silver nitrate=milliequivalents of thiocyanate
$$(ml_1)\,(N_1)=(ml_2)\,(N_2)$$

solve for N_2, the normality of the thiocyanate, as follows:

$$N_2 = \frac{(ml_1)(N_1)}{(ml\ of\ thiocyanate)}$$

Example:

$$N_2 = \frac{(35)(.1)}{(17.5)}$$

$$N_2 = \quad .2$$

STEP 2: DETERMINATION OF SILVER NITRATE CONCENTRATION

Determine the silver nitrate concentration by titrating the standardized thiocyanate solution into a sample of the silver bath as follows:

> **1.** Put 10 ml of the silver nitrate bath into a flask. A pipet or a 10 ml cylinder graduate may be used to measure the solution.

166   THE ALBUMEN & SALTED PAPER BOOK

2. Add 5 ml of 6 Molar nitric acid.

3. Add 1 ml of saturated ferric ammonium sulfate solution.

4. Run in the standardized thiocyanate solution from a buret into the silver nitrate sample until the faint brownish color will not disappear under vigorous stirring. To increase the detectability of the color, view the flask against a white background. Note the volume of thiocyanate titrated when the color first becomes permanent, then continue adding thiocyanate drop by drop to make sure.

5. Calculate the normality of the silver bath as follows:

$$\text{normality of silver nitrate} = \frac{(\text{ml of thiocyanate}) \, (\text{normality of thiocyanate})}{(\text{ml of silver nitrate in sample})}$$

6. To obtain the concentration of silver nitrate in the bath, multiply the normality of the silver nitrate by 170 (the molecular weight of silver nitrate). The result is expressed in grams per liter.

Example:

If the normality of the silver nitrate is .65N, then:

$$.65(170) = 110.5 \text{ g/liter}$$
$$110.5 \text{ g/liter} = 11.05\% \text{ silver nitrate solution}$$

7. For greater accuracy the titration procedure may be repeated and the two readings averaged together.

STEP 3: REPLENISHMENT OF THE SILVER BATH

The amount of silver nitrate required to restore the bath to proper strength will of course depend on the total volume of solution. For example, if after a titration the solution is found to be 8.5% in strength instead of 10% and possesses a total volume of 2 liters, the first step is to calculate how many grams per liter are lacking. In this case instead of 100 g/liter, there are only 85 g/liter, so 15 g/liter are missing. Multiply the number of missing grams/liter times the total number of liters of solution to find the amount of silver nitrate needed to replenish the solution:

$$15 \text{ g (2 liters)} = 30 \text{ g needed for replenishment}$$

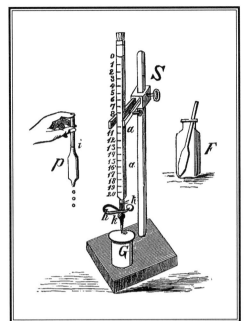

Helpful Hints for the Titration Procedure

1. Because thiocyanate solutions keep well, it is convenient to make up a large quantity of standardized solution. The ferric ammonium sulfate and nitric acid stock solutions will also keep well. Nitric acid should be stored in a ground-stoppered glass bottle.

2. Do not pour the thiocyanate solution that remains in the buret after a titration back into the container of standardized stock solution—throw it out.

3. Instead of calculating the normality each time a titration is performed, it is helpful to make a chart for each batch of standardized thiocyanate solution. The chart can be made by calculating a few points and drawing a line through the points. Label one axis of the graph in ml of standardized thiocyanate solution and the other in g/liter silver nitrate.

4. For increased economy a 5 ml sample of silver nitrate bath can be used without sacrificing accuracy, providing the sample is carefully measured out.

APPENDIX C

Introduction

It is a very difficult task to set forth guidelines for the identification of these materials because they are for the most part hand-crafted products; on the other hand, there do exist a few standard indicators that will yield a fairly reliable judgment. In the final analysis, process identification of 19th-century print materials depends almost wholly on experience and judgment, and is a skill that slowly improves with practice. The information presented here is intended solely to assist persons who may be unfamiliar with these materials in narrowing the range of possible choices, not in making positive identification of individual prints.

In order to develop skills in identifying albumen and salted paper prints, original prints must be seen and handled. In the case of salted paper prints this may not be easy, but sizeable photographic collections exist in every large city, and they are likely places to begin a process of familiarization. With regard to albumen prints, it is certainly very easy to find prints for study, although one must be sure that example prints are correctly labeled. Quite a few 19th-century journals contain tipped-in specimens of photographic prints of various kinds, and these prints are usually labeled as to process. Among the journals whose issues occasionally contained actual photographs are *The Photographic and Fine Art Journal, Anthony's Photographic Bulletin, Wilson's Photographic Magazine, The Philadelphia Photographer, Photographische Korrespondenz, Photographische Archiv,* and *The American Journal of Photography.* Specimen prints in journals are a particularly good way to help differentiate albumen paper from the gelatin and collodion printing-out papers which replaced it in photographic practice.

For those who are so inclined, an excellent way to develop skills in print identification is to actually make albumen and salted paper prints. A little direct experience with albumen will make it much more familiar when encountered in historical materials. The most important advice on the whole subject of identification, however, is not to rely on reproductions or descriptions of anything, but to seek out original materials and get to know them in all their variety.

Guidelines

I. IS THE PRINT A SILVER PHOTOGRAPHIC PRINT?

Silver photographic prints from the albumen and salted paper era (1840-1895) generally show some form of deterioration, or possess spots and blemishes of chemical origin that distinguish them as actual photographic prints. Most albumen and salted paper prints are faded and yellowed to some degree, either overall or in localized areas. A perfectly intact, unblemished image usually indicates that a print is not an albumen and salted paper print. Such a perfect print may either be of photomechanical origin, such as a woodburytype, carbon print, collotype, etc., or else may be a silver photographic print on gelatin or collodion printing-out paper. These materials may resemble albumen prints, but have generally survived in better condition.

II. DOES THE PRINT DISPLAY THE CHARACTERISTIC COLORS OF ALBUMEN AND SALTED PAPERS PRINTS?

Image color is one of the most important factors in identifying albumen and salted paper prints, but it is also an area where experience is vitally necessary. In light of this fact a list of possible image colors is of very limited value. A discussion of image color is complicated by the problem of changes induced in prints by fading and yellowing, and also by the fact that many photomechanical processes could (and did) successfully mimic the color and appearance of albumen prints. A third complicating factor is the possibility that a print was hand colored using water colors or aniline dyes.

Albumen and salted paper prints in original condition are usually warm brown, purplish-brown, purple or purplish-black. They are seldom black, but occasionally they will approach neutral black yet still contain some trace of purple in middletone areas. They are never green, but severely faded and yellowed albumen prints sometimes possess a faint greenish tinge. Approximately 85% of albumen prints show some readily noticeable yellow or yellowish-brown stain in the whites and highlight areas. The presence of highlight yellowing and the characteristic surface texture of albumen are two of the most readily apparent and reliable indicators that a given print is an albumen print. Albumen prints are certainly not the only types of prints that may exhibit highlight yellowing, however, so one must also watch for contraindications that may be present.

III. WHAT ARE THE SURFACE CHARACTERISTICS OF THE PRINT?

Surface characteristics by themselves are little help in differentiating albumen and salted paper prints from other kinds of photographic prints; corroborating indicators must also be present. Many photographic materials have similar surface qualities and the appearance of any surface may be altered by smoothing or the application of other substances. Nevertheless the basic fact remains that salted paper prints are rough or matte-surfaced, while albumen prints are smooth and display a greater or lesser degree of surface gloss. Salted paper prints were made on both smooth and porous rawstocks of various weights, but albumen prints (especially after 1860) were generally made on a very smooth, lightweight stock. Albumen prints of the period 1850-1870 are usually less glossy than those of the period 1870-1890, because of two factors: the use of burnishing and rolling machines to smooth the prints after mounting, and the increased use after 1870 of double-coated paper.

Albumen paper was not made with a substratum of barium sulfate (baryta) and gelatin as were emulsion-type gelatin and collodion printing-out papers, and therefore these materials exhibit a generally smoother surface than albumen prints. Albumen paper usually exhibits a characteristic surface texture which (if not obscured by burnishing or rolling) sometimes possesses a "crackled" or "crazed" appearance. Experienced individuals usually have little difficulty in detecting albumen paper by its surface texture.

IV. CAN THE IMAGE BE DATED FROM INTERNAL EVIDENCE?

Information contained in the photographic image itself or on the mount of the photograph can often help to establish the approximate time at which the negative or print was made. Only in rare instances will there be a significant lag between the making of the negative and the making of the print, so it can be assumed in most cases that the negative and the print have the same approximate date of origin. There are many internal clues to aid in the dating of a photograph, and assigning an approximate date is a common practice in historical photographic collections.

Once it has been established that a print is a silver photographic print and an approximate date has been determined for it, reference to the chart below may be helpful in process identification:

MOST COMMON TYPES OF PHOTOGRAPHIC PAPER, 1840-1905

1840-1855	Salted Papers
1855-1895	Albumen Paper
1895-1905	Gelatin and Collodion Printing-out Papers

Within the span 1840-1905 there are obviously periods of transition from one type of printing paper to another, and in these transition periods the date of origin of an image is not much help in identifying the specific print process. On the other hand, there are also spans of time where there can be little doubt as to the printing paper in use by the vast majority of photographers. One such time is of course the 10-year period between 1840 and 1850, before the invention of albumen paper. Except for very rare cases where the prints were made by development (using the calotype, or paper negative process), prints of this decade are plain salted paper prints.

The years 1850-1860 represent a transition period between salted papers and albumen paper. For the first few years of the decade plain salted papers predominated, while at mid-decade came a time of unprecedented variety, as albumen paper coexisted with a number of different kinds of matte salted papers. These matte salted papers were treated with a salting-sizing solution using an organic binder such as gelatin, whey or starch, among other substances. It is not possible to differentiate at a glance between these various types of matte salted paper. As the year 1860 drew closer, albumen paper gradually replaced most of the varieties of salted papers, and ascended to an almost unchallenged dominance of photographic practice.

Thus the period 1860-1885 is a time of reasonable certainty with regard to process identity, and there is a great likelihood that any given silver photographic print of that period was made on albumen paper. Studio portraits (except life-size enlargements) and stereo views of this era are especially likely to be albumen prints, and indeed photographs of any kind from this period *not* made on albumen paper are unusual. After 1885 an enormous number of photographs were produced on albumen paper, but there can be little certainty in a process identification based on the date of the photograph. The mid-1880's began a 30-year period of great diversity in photographic printing papers. World War I marked the end of this era of diversity, and consolidated the dominance of develop-out bromide and chlorobromide papers, a dominance which lasted until the early 1960's. At that time chromogenic color papers became the most widely used photographic printing material and have remained so until the present day.

V. RESOURCES WHICH MAY ASSIST IN PROCESS IDENTIFICATION

Arthur T. Gill, *Photographic Processes, a Glossary and Chart for Recognition,* Museums Association Information Sheet IS No. 21, 1978. Published by the Museums Association, 87 Charlotte St., London W1P 2BX, United Kingdom

Siegfried Rempel, *The Care of Black and White Photographic Collections: Identification of Processes,* Technical Bulletin No. 6, published by The Canadian Conservation Institute, National Museums Canada. Technical Bulletins may be requested free of charge by writing the Canadian Conservation Institute, 1030 Innes Road, Ottawa, Ontario, Canada K1A 0M8

There are two very useful web resources for process identification. One is the Image Permanence Institute's www.graphicsatlas.org. I believe the reader will find this an invaluable reference in both teaching and learning about many graphic and photographic processes. The other is http://albumen.conservation-us.org, a superb collection of knowledge and research about albumen prints.

REFERENCES

CHAPTER ONE: BASIC PRINCIPLES
1. J.M. Eder and Fritz Wentzel, *Die photographischen Kopirverfahren mit Silbersalzen (Positiv-Prozess)*, Wilhelm Knapp, Halle (1928), pp. v-vi.

CHAPTER TWO: WORKING ENVIRONMENT, EQUIPMENT & MATERIALS
1. Edward L. Wilson, *Wilson's Photographics*, pub. Edw. Wilson, New York (1881), p. 189.
2. J.M. Eder and Fritz Wentzel, *Die photographischen Kopirverfahren mit Silbersalzen (Positiv-Prozess)*, Wilhelm Knapp, Halle (1928), p. 110.
3. A. von Hübl, *Der Silberdruck auf Salzpapier*, Wilhelm Knapp, Halle (1896), p.31.

CHAPTER THREE: SALTED PAPERS
1. Thomas Sutton, "On Positive Printing, Etc.," *Photographic Journal*, 2, 311 (1856).
2. William Henry Fox Talbot, "Some Account of the Art of Photogenic Drawing, or the Process by which Natural Objects may be made to delineate themselves without the aid of the Artist's

Pencil," *The Athenaeum*, No. 539 (Feb. 9, 1839), p. 114.

3. W.H. Fox Talbot, "An Account of the Processes employed in Photogenic Drawing," *The Athenaeum*, No. 539 (Feb. 23, 1839), p. 156.

4. Louis Alphonse Davanne and Jules Girard, *Recherches Théoretiques et Pratiques sur la Formation des Épreuves Photographiques Positives*, Gauthier-Villars, Paris (1864), p. 3.

5. Paul E. Liesegang, *Der Silberdruck*, E. Liesegang's Verlag, Düsseldorf (1884), pp. 12-13.

6. J.M. Eder and Fritz Wentzel, *Die photographischen Kopirverfahren mit Silbersalzen (Positiv-Prozess)*, Wilhelm Knapp, Halle (1928), p. 185.

7. DeBrébisson, *Horn's Photographic Journal*, 2, 47 (1854).

CHAPTER FOUR: ALBUMEN PAPER

1. W.H. Sherman, "The Past and Future of the Albumen Print," in *The American Annual of Photography and Photographic Times Almanac*, Scovill & Adams, New York (1892), p. 25.

2. "H.L.," *The Athenaeum*, No. 602 (May 11, 1839), p. 358.

3. Robert Hunt, *A Popular Treatise on the Art of Photography*, Richard Griffin & Co., Glasgow (1841),p. 11.

4. J.M. Eder, *Die photographischen Kopirverfahren mit Silbersalzen (Positiv-Prozess)*, Wilhelm Knapp, Halle (1887), 1st edition, p. 30.

5. Julius Schnauss, "Economical Process for Printing Positives," *Photographic Mosaics*, Benerman & Wilson, Philadelphia (1867), pp. 65-67. Taken from *Photographisches Archiv* (1886), p. 45.

6. Louis-Désiré Blanquart-Evrard, *Compte Rendu Des Seances De L'Académie Des Sciences, 30 (21)*, 665 (1850).

7. *Die Photographische Industrie, 27*, 116 (1929).

8. *Liverpool Photographic Journal, 3*, 25 (1856). See also D. Van Monckhoven, *Traité Général de Photographic*, A Gaudin & Frére, Paris (1856), 2nd edition, p. 243.

9. *Anthony's Photographic Bulletin, 21*, 225 (1890). See also Edward L. Wilson, "Die Papierfabrik in Rives," *Photographische Mittheilungen, 19*, (1883).

10. Fritz Wentzel, *Memoirs of a Photochemist*, American Museum of Photography, Philadelphia(1960), pp. 51-52.

11. J.M. Eder, editor, *Jahrbuch für Photographic, Kinematographie und Reproduktionsverfahren*, Wilhelm Knapp, Halle (1905), p. 432.

12. J.M. Eder and Fritz Wentzel, *Die photographischen Kopirver-fahren mit Silbersalzen (Positiv-Prozess)*, Wilhelm Knapp, Halle (1928), p. 200.

13. Reese V. Jenkins, *Images and Enterprise: Technology and the American Photographic Industry 1839 to 1925*, Johns Hopkins University Press, Baltimore (1975), p. 49.

14. *Anthony's Photographic Bulletin, 21*, 225 (1890).

15. *British Journal of Photography, 36*, 390 (1889).

16. *Photographisches Archiv, 2*, 57 (1889).

17. J.M. Eder, *Die photographischen Kopirverfahren mit Silbersalzen (Positiv-Prozess)*, Wilhelm Knapp, Halle (1887), p. 71.

18. F. Wilde, "The Permanency of Photographs—Silver, Carbon and Platinum," *American Journal of Photography, 12 (134)*, 51 (1891).

19. *Photographisches Archiv, 2*, 57 (1889).

20. Henry C. Stiefel, *Sensitized Papers, How Made and Used*, The Adams Press, New York (1894), p. 29.

21. Hermann W. Vogel, *Handbook of the Practice and Art of Photography*, Benerman & Wilson, Philadelphia (1875), 2nd edition, pp. 179-180.

CHAPTER FIVE: ALTERNATIVE AND HYBRID PAPERS

1. *The British Journal of Photography Almanac and Photographer's Daily Companion*, H. Greenwood & Co., London (1912), p. 1035.

2. Marcus Sparling, *Theory and Practice of the Photographic Art*, Houlston & Stoneman, London (1856), pp. 155-156.

3. J.M. Eder and Fritz Wentzel, *Die photographischen Kopirver-fahren mit Silbersalzen (Positiv-Prozess)*, Wilhelm Knapp, Halle (1928), pp. 192-194.

4. H. Snowden Ward, ed., *The Figures, Facts and Formulae of Photography*, Tennant & Ward, New York (1904), 3rd edition, pp. 74-75. See also A. von Hübl, *Der Silberdruck auf Salzpapier*, Wilhelm Knapp, Halle (1896), p. 71.

5. W.K. Burton and Andrew Pringle, *The Processes of Pure Photography*, Scovill & Adams, New York (1889), p. 138.

6. *The Photographic Journal, 3*, 40 (1856). See also J.M. Eder and Fritz Wentzel, *Die photographischen Kopirverfahren mit Silbersalzen (Positiv-Prozess)*, Wilhelm Knapp, Halle (1928), p. 187.

7. H.P. Robinson and William DeW. Abney, *The Art and Practice of Silver Printing*, E. & H.T. Anthony, New York (1881), pp. 100-102.

8. J.M. Eder, *Die photographischen Kopirverfahren mit Silbersalzen (Positiv-Prozess)*, Wilhelm Knapp, Halle (1887), 1st edition, pp. 8-9.

9. George Shadbolt, "Some Observations on Positive Printing," *Photographic Journal*, 2, 256-257 (1855).

10. J.M. Eder, ed., *Jahrbuch für Photographic und Reproduktionstechnik*, Wilhelm Knapp, Halle (1891), p. 519.

11. J.M. Eder, ed., *Jahrbuch für Photographic, Kinematographie und Reproduktionsverfahren*, Wilhelm Knapp, Halle (1911), p. 529.

12. K. Kieser, *Photographische Papiere*, Urban & Schwarzenberg, Berlin (1931), pp. 45 7-458.

13. H.P. Robinson and William DeW. Abney, *The Art and Practice of Silver Printing*, E. & H.T. Anthony, New York (1881), p. 101.

14. A. von Hübl, *Der Silberdruck auf Salzpapier*, Wilhelm Knapp, Halle (1896), pp. 78-79.

15. J.M. Eder, ed., *Jahrbuch für Photographic und Reproduktionstechnik*, Wilhelm Knapp, Halle (1898), p.437.

16. Fritz Wentzel, *Memoirs of a Photochemist*, American Museum of Photography, Philadelphia (1960), p. 69.

17. *Die Photographische Industrie*, 11, 802 (1913).

18. *The British Journal Almanac and Photographer's Daily Companion*, H. Longwood & Co., London (1912), p. 1035. See also *Photo Gazette* (Paris), April 27, 1909.

19. Die Photographische Industrie, 27, 116 (1929).

20. A. von Hübl, *Der Silberdruck auf Salzpapier*, Wilhelm Knapp, Halle (1896), pp. 82-83.

21. *Die Photographische Industrie*, 11, 503 (1913).

CHAPTER SIX: SENSITIZATION

1. C.A. Seely, "The Use of Acid in Silver Printing Solutions," *The Photographic News*, 3, (67), 173 (1860).

2. A. von Hübl, *Der Silberdruck auf Salzpapier*, Wilhelm Knapp, Halle (1896), p. 34.

3. "R . ," "Printing and Toning on Albumenised Paper," *The Photographic News, 3 (70)*, 206 (1860).

4. J.M. Eder and Fritz Wentzel, *Die photographischen Kopriverfahren mit Silbersalzen (Positiv-Prozess)*, Wilhelm Knapp, Halle (1928), p. 199.

5. *The Photographic Times 2*, 88 (1872). A sample print made on "ready-sensitized paper" accompanied this issue of the journal.

6. Josef Maria Eder, *The History of Photography*, trans. Edward Epstean, Columbia University Press, New York (1945), p. 534.

7. Charles W. Hearn, *The Practical Printer*, Benerman & Wilson, Philadelphia (1874), p. 24.

CHAPTER SEVEN: TONE REPRODUCTION AND PRINT EXPOSURE
1. Thomas Bolas, *Photographic Review, 1*, 219 (1889).
2. A. von Hübl, *Der Silberdruck auf Salzpapier,* Wilhelm Knapp, Halle (1896), p. 4.
3. *Ibid.,* p. 5.
4. J.M. Eder and Fritz Wentzel, *Die photographischen Kopirverfahren mit Silbersalzen (Positiv-Prozess),* Wilhelm Knapp, Halle (1928), pp. 88-89.

CHAPTER EIGHT: TONING
1. Fitt, "On Positive Printing," *Liverpool Photographic Journal, 3,* 36 (1856).
2. Brian W. Coe, "Sun Pictures: Printing Talbot's Calotype Negatives," *History of Photography, 1 (3),* 180 (1977).
3. J.M. Eder and Fritz Wentzel, *Die photographischen Kopirverfahren mit Silbersalzen (Positiv-Prozess),* Wilhelm Knapp, Halle (1928), p. 8.
4. P. Mercier, *Virages et Fixages,* Gauthier-Villars, Paris (1892), p. 8.
5. *Ibid.,* p.6.
6. P.F. Mathieu, *Auto-Photographic ou Méthode De Reproduction Par La Lumière des Dessins, Lithographs, Gravures, etc., Sans L'Emploi Du Daguerréotype,* Imprimerie De Bureau, Paris (1847), p. 14.
7. *American Journal of Photography, 2,* 270(1860).
8. "R.," "Printing and Toning on Albumenised Paper," *The Photographic News, 3 (70),* 205 (1860).
9. P. Mercier, *Virages et Fixages,* Gauthier-Villars, Paris (1892), p. 16.
10. Chapman Jones, "On the Relationship Between the Size of the Particle and the Colour of the Image," *Photographic Journal, 51,* 162 (1911).
11. E. Weyde, E. Klein and H.J. Metz, "Silver Deposition in the Diffusion Process," *Journal of Photographic Science, 10,* 112 (1962).
12. G. Mie, *Annalen der Physik, 25,* 377 (1908).
13. J.M. Eder and Fritz Wentzel, *Die photographischen Kopirverfahren mit Silbersalzen (Positiv-Prozess),* Wilhelm Knapp, Halle (1928), pp. 41-43.
14. Edward L. Wilson, *Wilson's Photographics,* pub. Edward L. Wilson, New York (1881), p. 202.
15. P. Mercier, *Virages et Fixages,* Gauthier-Villars, Paris (1892), p. 15.

16. J.M. Eder and Fritz Wentzel, *Die photographischen Kopirverfahren mit Silbersalzen (Positiv-Prozess)*, Wilhelm Knapp, Halle (1928), pp. 63-64.
17. *Ibid.*, p. 13.
18. Alfred Stieglitz, "Toning Aristo Prints with Platinum," *American Annual of Photography and Photographic Times Almanac*, Scovill & Adams, New York (1890), p. 120.

CHAPTER NINE: FIXATION AND WASHING

1. A. Haddon and F.B. Grundy, "Strength of Hypo Solution and Times of Immersion for Fixing Albumenised Paper," *British Journal of Photography*, 44, 173 (1897).
2. Beaumont Newhall, *Latent Image*, Doubleday, New York (1967), p. 58.
3. G.I.P. Levenson, *Theory of the Photographic Process*, ed. T.H. James, MacMillan, New York (1977), p. 439.
4. *Ibid.*, p. 457.
5. J.M. Eder and Fritz Wentzel, *Die photographischen Kopirverfahren mit Silbersalzen (Positiv-Prozess)*, Wilhelm Knapp, Halle (1928), p. 80.
6. L. P. Clerc, *Photography, Theory and Practice*, Pitman, New York (1939), 2nd edition, p. 346.
7. Walter Meidinger, *Die Theoretischen Grundlagen der Photographischen Prozesse*, Verlag von Julius Springer, Vienna (1932), p. 431.
8. J.I. Crabtree, G.T. Eaton and L.E. Muehler, *Photographic Journal*, 80, 458 (1940).
9. H.P. Robinson and William DeW. Abney, *The Art and Practice of Silver Printing*, E. & H.T. Anthony, New York (1881), p. 95.
10. F.B. Grundy and A. Haddon, "On the Amounts of Silver and Hypo Left in Albumenised Paper at Different Stages of Washing," *British Journal of Photography*, 40, 512 (1893).

CHAPTER TEN: FINISHING, MOUNTING AND STORAGE

1. Thomas F. Hardwich, *Photographic Journal*, 3, 43 (1856).
2. Edward L. Wilson, *Wilson's Photographics*, pub. Edward L. Wilson, New York (1881), p. 235.
3. *Photographic Journal*, 2, 252 (1855).
4. Paul E. Liesegang, *Der Silberdruck*, E. Liesegang's Verlag, Düsseldorf (1884), p. 59.
5. John Towler, *The Silver Sunbeam*, Joseph Ladd, New York (1864), p. 206.

6. Robert Howlett, *On the Various Methods of Printing Photographic Pictures Upon Paper,* Sampson, Low & Marston, London (1856), p. 32.

7. J.G. Tunny, in *Wilson's Photographics,* pub. Edward L. Wilson, New York(1881), p. 234.

8. Lucia C. Tang, "Determination of Iron and Copper in 18th and 19th Century Books by Flameless Atomic Absorption Spectroscopy," *Journal of the American Institute for Conservation, 17,* 19 (1978).

9. Edith Weyde, "A Simple Test to Identify Gases Which Destroy Silver Images," *Photographic Science and Engineering, 16 (4),* 286 (1972).

CHAPTER ELEVEN: THE QUESTION OF PERMANENCE

1. Edgar Clifton, "The Last Print in Silver," *British Journal of Photography Almanac and Photographer's Daily Companion,* H. Greenwood & Co., London (1887), p.137.

2. Helmut and Alison Gernsheim, *The History of Photography,* McGraw-Hill, New York (1969), p. 175.

3. Nikolaas Henneman, *Photographic Journal 3,* 43 (1856). For a detailed account by Thomas Malone of the making of *The Pencil of Nature* prints, see *The Liverpool and Manchester Photographic Journal, 1,* 270 (1857).

4. T.F. Hardwich, *Photographic Journal, 2,* 242 (1855).

5. *Photographic Journal, 2,* 251 (1855).

6. Alphonse Davanne and Jules Girard, *Photographic Journal, 2,* 202 (1855), from *Bulletin De La Société De Photographie,* June 1855.

7. Ralph E. Liesegang, *Photographische Physik,* E. Liesegang's Verlag, Düsseldorf (1899), p. 36. See also *British Journal of Photography, 26,* 2 (1879).

8. W.H. Sherman, "The Past and Future of Albumen Print," *American Annual of Photography* and *The Photographic Times Almanac,* Scovill & Adams, New York (1892), p. 23.

9. Reese V. Jenkins, *Images and Enterprise: Technology and The American Photographic Industry 1839-1925,* John Hopkins University Press, Baltimore (1975), pp. 90-95.

10. Alphonse Davanne and Jules Girard, *Bulletin De La Société Française De Photographie, 5,* 347 (1859).

11. Alphonse Davanne and Jules Girard, "General Observations on Photographic Positives," *The Photographic News, 3,* 233 (1860).

12. Matthew Carey Lea, "An Examination Into the Circumstances

Under Which Silver is Found in the Whites of Albumen Prints," *The Photographic News*, 10, 394-395 (1866) and 10, 402-403 (1866).

13. John Spiller, quoted by A. Haddon and F.B. Grundy in *British Journal of Photography*, 40, 511-512 (1893).

14. F.B. Grundy and A. Haddon, "On the Amounts of Silver and Hypo Left in Albumenised Paper at Different Stages of Washing," *British Journal of Photography*, 40, 512 (1893).

15. *British Journal of Photography*, 40, 511-512 (1893), 41, 788-789 (1894), and 43, 468-469 (1896).

APPENDIX A: FURTHER READING

1. Henry Morley and W.H. Wills, "Photography," *Household Words, New Series 1 (28)*, 57 (1853). Authorship of this unsigned article was ascribed to Morley and Wills by R.D. Wood in the 1975 pamphlet, *The Calotype Patent Lawsuit of Talbot vs. Laroche 1854*, p. 28.

REFERENCES
FOR ILLUSTRATIONS

Acknowledgement

The author wishes to thank those people and institutions which assisted him in locating and reproducing the illustrations for this book. Thanks are due to Robert Bretz, librarian at The Visual Studies Workshop, Rochester, New York, to Gladys Taylor, archivist at Rochester Institute of Technology, to Jeffrey Wolin, director of re-production services and Susan Wyngaard, director of the research center at George Eastman House, and also to Prof. Joseph Noga of the School of Printing, Rochester Institute of Technology. The per-mission of the institutions named above to reproduce the illustra-tions is also gratefully acknowledged.

Fig. 1.   J.M. Eder, *Die photographischen Copirverfahren mit Silber-salzen (Positiv-Prozess)*, Wilhelm Knapp, Halle (1893), p. 103.

Fig. 2.   Alfred Watkins, *The Watkins Manual*, Hereford (1903), 2nd ed., p. 126.

Fig. 3.   Charles W. Hearn, *The Practical Printer*, pub. Edward L. Wilson, Philadelphia (1878), 2nd ed., p. 16.

Fig. 4.   W. Jerome Harrison, *The Chemistry of Photography*, Scovill & Adams, New York (1892), p.44.

Fig. 5.   W. I. Scandlin, ed., *The International Annual of Anthony's Photographic Bulletin and American Process Year-Book, 1901*, E. & H. T. Anthony, New York (1901), adv. p. 1.

Fig. 6.   A. H. Elliott and F. P. Smith, eds., *The International Annual of Anthony's Photographic Bulletin, 1894*, E. & H. T. Anthony, New York (1894), adv. p. 58.

Fig. 7.   Alexander Watt, *The Art of Papermaking*, Crosby Lockwood & Son, London (1901), 2nd ed., p.23.

Fig. 8.   Harry R. Lewis, *Productive Poultry Husbandry*, J. P. Lippincott, Philadelphia (1913), p. 78.

Fig. 9.   *The Magazine of Science and School of Arts*, Vol. 4, No. 1 (April 27, 1839).

Fig. 10.   J.M. Eder, *Der Collodion und Daguerreotyp-Process, und ältere Negativ-Processe*, Wilhelm Knapp, Halle (1893), p. 84.

Fig. 11.   *Ibid.*, p. 85.

Fig. 12.   J.M. Eder, *Die photographischen Copirverfahren mit Silber-salzen (Positiv-Prozess)*, Wilhelm Knapp, Halle (1893), p. 120.

Fig. 13.   H. Baden Pritchard, ed., *The Year Book of Photography and Photographic News Almanac, 1885*, Piper and Carter, London (1885), p. 1x.

Fig. 14.   Giuseppe Pizzighelli, *Anleitung Zur Photographie,* Wilhelm Knapp, Halle (1914), 2nd ed., p. 404.

Fig. 15.   J.M. Eder, *Die photographischen Copirverfahren mit Silbersalzen (Positiv-Prozess),* Wilhelm Knapp, Halle (1898), p. 121.

Fig. 16.   *Ibid.,* p. 121.

Fig. 17.   *Ibid.,* p. 122.

Fig. 18.   *Ibid.,* p. 123.

Fig. 19.   *Ibid.,* p. 123.

Fig. 20.   *Ibid.,* p. 124.

Fig. 21.   *The Photographic News, 1 (12),* 119 (1858).

Fig. 22.   Charles W. Hearn, *The Practical Printer,* pub. Edward L. Wilson, Philadelphia (1874), p. 202.

Fig. 23.   J.M. Eder, *Die photographischen Copirverfahren mit Silbersalzen (Positiv Prozess),* Wilhelm Knapp, Halle (1893), p. 73.

Fig. 24.   W. I. Lincoln Adams, ed., *The American Annual of Photography and Photographic Times Almanac, 1894,* Scovill & Adams, New York (1894), p.13.

Fig. 25.   W. B. Bolton, ed., *The British Journal Photographic Almanac and Photographer's Daily Companion for 1882,* H. Greenwood, London (1882), p. cxxxvi.

Fig. 26.   *Photographic Mosaics,* Edward L. Wilson, pub., Philadelphia (1878), p. 100.

Fig. 27.   *Paris Photo-Gazette,* April 25, 1909, p. xiv.

Fig. 28.   Edward L. Wilson, *Wilson's Quarter Century in Photography,* pub. Edward L. Wilson, New York (1887), p. 449.

Fig. 29.   Charles W. Hearn, *The Practical Printer,* pub. Edward L. Wilson, Philadelphia (1878) 2nd ed., p. 18.

Fig. 30. Matthew Carey Lea, *A Manual of Photography,* privately printed, Philadelphia (1871), 2nd ed., p. 145.

Fig. 31. J. Traill Taylor, ed., *The British Journal Almanac and Photographer's Daily Companion for 1887,* Henry Greenwood & Co., London (1887), adv. p. ccviii.

Fig. 32. J.M. Eder, *Das Atelier und Laboratorium des Photographen,* Wilhelm Knapp, Halle (1893), p.47.

Fig. 33. Hermann W. Vogel, *Handbuch der Photographic, Part III, Section II. Die Photographischen Copirverfahren mit Silber, Eisen, Chrom und Uransalzen,* Gustav Schmidt, Berlin (1889), p. 34.

Fig. 34. J.M. Eder, *Das Atelier und Laboratorium des Photographen,* Wilhelm Knapp, Halle (1893), p. 48.

Fig. 35. *Ibid.,* p. 47.

Fig. 36. Andrew Pringle, *Practical Photomicrography,* Scovill & Adams, New York (1890), p. 117.

Fig. 37. Charles W. Hearn, *The Practical Printer,* pub. Edward L. Wilson, Philadelphia (1878), 2nd ed., p. 17.

Fig. 38. J.M. Eder, *Die photographischen Copirverfahren mit Silbersalzen (Positiv-Prozess),* Wilhelm Knapp, Halle (1893), p. 126.

Fig. 39. Elbert Anderson, *The Skylight and the Dark-Room,* Benerman & Wilson, Philadelphia (1872), p. 165.

Fig. 40. M. Albert, *La Photographic Moderne,* G. Masson, Paris (1896), p. 442.

Fig. 41. H. J. Rodgers, *Twenty-Three Years Under a Skylight,* pub. H. J. Rodgers, Hartford (1872), errata page.

Fig. 42. J.M. Eder, *Die photographischen Copirverfahren mit Silbersalzen (Positiv-Prozess),* Wilhelm Knapp, Halle (1893), p. 136.

Fig. 43.   A. H. Elliott and F. P. Smith, eds., *The International Annual of Anthony's Photographic Bulletin, 1894,* E. & H. T. Anthony, New York (1894), adv. p.75.

Fig. 44.   H. Baden Pritchard, ed., *The Year Book of Photography and Photographic News Almanac, 1884,* Piper & Carter, London (1884), front advertising pages.

Fig. 45.   J.M. Eder, *Die photographischen Copirverfahren mit Silbersalzen (Positiv-Prozess),* Wilhelm Knapp, Halle (1893), p. 142.

Fig. 46.   P. H. Emerson, *Naturalistic Photography for Students of the Art,* Scovill & Adams, New York (1899), p.281.

Fig. 47.   Edward L. Wilson, *Wilson's Quarter Century in Photography,* pub. Edward L. Wilson, New York (1887), p. 281.